RUNNING TO MYSELF

A Journey of Endurance

Acyr da Luz

Edited by Joe Pierson and Lindsey Alexander
Cover and interior design by David Provolo

ISBN: 979-8-9989854-0-9 (paperback color)
ISBN: 979-8-9989854-1-6 (hardcover color)

CONTENTS

Chapter 1

No Easy Day

"Enthusiasm is common. Endurance is rare."
—*Angela Duckworth, American academic and psychologist*

2019

I opened my eyes, and everything was still pitch black. I was not sure where I was. I felt awake, alert, but lost. It was as if I were in another place before and suddenly woke up there, in that strange room. My wife was sleeping by my side, but that was not the right side of the bed. What was going on? I started searching for my phone to turn on the flashlight, and just as I found it, the alarm went off. It was 4 a.m. I quickly turned it off, but the split second that it rang was enough to wake up my wife, who, half asleep, or more precisely, 99 percent asleep, asked me, "Are you feeling better?"

"Yes, I'm fine," I replied while sitting on the side of the bed, trying to make sense of what was happening. Sitting proved to be much harder than I thought. I was stiff and sore. My legs, back, shoulders, neck, and everything in between screamed in pain. While I was still trying to make sense of what was going on, my wife, wearing an expression that was a mixture of relief and worry, asked me, "So, are you 'fine' enough for day two?"

I switched on my cell phone. I was confused, so I used the cell phone flashlight to illuminate the cozy room we were staying in. As my surroundings came into focus, it all came back to me.

We were at a nice house in the city of Penticton, the triathlon capital of Canada. My wife was referring to day two of the Ultraman Canada Race, a grueling ultra-distance triathlon that takes place over the summer. And what a summer it was. To my surprise, and for most people not that familiar with British Columbia, it is the hottest area in Canada. The temperatures during summer may reach 113º F (45º C), which was exactly what had happened the day before, on day one of Ultraman Canada 2019, and it really hit me hard. After swimming 6.2 miles on Okanagan Lake, home of the famous Ogopogo (the Canadian version of the Loch Ness Monster), and riding ninety miles in an oven-like atmosphere, I finished day one in horrible physical condition. By the end of the day, I was battling a heatstroke and a high fever. Things were not looking good, but I had my crew to help me.

In the Ultraman, each athlete has to have their own crew that provides food, water, directions, and anything that the athlete may need during the race. Their crew is the soul of each athlete. My crew comprised my wife, Jaína (Jai), our kids, Sophia (Sol) and Gabriel (Gabe), who were twelve and seven at that time, my sister Tatiana (Tata), and my good friend Yonathan (Yon). They all traveled to Canada to spend three days following me around, crammed in a van, while I would swim 6.2 miles, bike 261.5 miles, and run 52.2 miles over the course of three days. All these people took three full days, not counting the travel days, to help me complete one of the hardest triathlons in the world.

As soon as I arrived back at the house where we were staying from day one, I took a long cold shower. I really needed to cool down. I then walked to the kitchen, where Yon was finalizing dinner, a fresh salmon cooked with rice and salad. Tata was preparing the sandwiches and snacks for the next day, and Jai was preparing dinner for the kids.

I wanted to help them, but I had no strength left to do so. I didn't even have the strength to eat Yon's carefully prepared dinner. I needed to eat; everyone reminded me all the time that I needed to eat, but I just couldn't. I looked at my wife and said, "Please prepare the kids. I don't think tomorrow will really happen and they will be …"

My sister interrupted me. "Don't get ahead of yourself; just take some rest. I know you, just go to bed. I'm sure you will pass out for a couple of hours and be fresh tomorrow. All of us people that have normal sleep patterns will be the ones struggling!"

With no ability to argue, I just went to bed. My wife came to help me. She put a bucket close by in case I felt sick during the night, helped manage my body temperature with some wet towels, and this is the last thing I remembered from that night.

While everything was connecting in my brain, Jai asked again, "So, will you do it or not? We already prepared the kids, saying that this is a hard race and completing day one on the first attempt was already a big victory …"

I interrupted her and quickly replied, "Yes, I'm going to do it."

The only thing worse than the pain in that moment was the doubt. *Could I really do it? Should I really do it? Why did I sign up for such a crazy thing?* My body wanted a break. I wanted a break. I could not let anyone, not even Jai, give me an easy way out; I had to complete what I had signed up to do.

Jai looked at me, now with her eyes opened, and by her voice, I could tell that my answer woke her up. "Do you know, Tata was right!"

I got off the bed and went for a hot shower to warm my body and loosen the muscles, while Jai went to wake up Yon and Tata. Day one was not only hard for me, but it was also extremely hard for my crew too, especially because we were all caught by surprise at how exhausting the whole experience was. When I signed up, I told my wife that she would have to be my support during the swim; she would have to kayak

6.2 miles, and after that, they could enjoy the beautiful region around Penticton. They could spend time at the wineries and meet me every four to six hours to refill my water bottles and food. I could not be more wrong. The only fun part of crewing was probably the "plank challenge" competition going on with the other crews; despite that, crewing on an ultra-triathlon was intense, stressful, and required experience, which none of us had.

Right after the shower, I went to check the bike. I had a flat tire the day before, for which I had switched my racing wheel to a spare one, but I still had to resolve the puncture on the race wheel tire, as it was a much faster wheel/tire combination. Moreover, I didn't want to go for day two without a proper spare wheel. No one in my crew knew how to fix a flat tire, or at least that was what I thought.

When I arrived at the bike, the tire was fixed, and the bike was ready with the right wheels and tires. A few minutes later, Yon arrived and said, "You are good to go. I fixed the tire, checked the other tire, and everything is ready to roll. I knew you would race today!"

It was a pleasant surprise.

It was 6 a.m., time to leave the house, but the kids were still sleeping, and Jai and Tata were far from ready. They were working on all the preparation, and of course, it was much more complicated than we thought. They had to prepare the food, water, supplies, and everything that five normal people would need during the day and all the special supplies that a not-so-normal person would need to bike 171.5 miles. Yes, you read it correctly, I had 171.5 miles of biking ahead of me, in the heat and over what I thought was the most difficult part, with over six thousand feet of elevation, similar to the highest peak in Brazil, where I come from. With the time pressure, we decided to split. Yon went with me to the starting line. Jai and Tata stayed back home getting everyone and everything ready for the day.

During the drive to the starting line, Yon asked me, "Do you remember what you said yesterday, right after crossing the finish line, while you were giving me your bike?"

I was puzzled and could not remember. I shook my head.

Yon continued, "You said, 'This was the easy day!'"

Then I nodded. I could remember what had happened after he told me. When planning for the race, I always thought day two would be the hardest, not because of the distance but because of the cutoff time. I had to complete the 171.5 miles in less than twelve hours, which I knew would be extremely hard due to all the elevation. Day three was the second hardest because running a double marathon seems impossible by itself. Imagine doing that after all the effort of the first two days. Day one was different. As a decent swimmer, I expected to finish the 6.2-mile swim way ahead of the six-hour cutoff time and then to take it easy on the bike to complete the ninety miles well within the twelve hours. Therefore, it got the nickname of "the easy day." Reality was vastly different. The heat was brutal, and I almost didn't complete it. An Ultraman has no easy day.

Yon and I were among the first ones to arrive at the starting line. I took the bike off the car and started to slowly assemble everything, then someone stopped by and told us that we needed to move to the parking lot next to the one we were in. Without hesitation, I told Yon to drive there and that I'd bike. Mounting on the bike was hard. My body was aching. Riding to the next parking lot was terrible; my body was a wreck! How could I ride 171.5 miles at a frenetic pace if I could not even manage to move my bike from one parking lot to the next?

About thirty minutes later, the race officials called all of us. It was time to line up for the start of the big day. Quitting before it started was not an option. I stopped some stretches I was doing and got myself in line. At 7 a.m., the gun went off. It was time to start. I'm not sure if it was the adrenaline, the caffeinated breakfast, the stretches, or just the shame of quitting in front of all those people, but something got me going, and I started surprisingly well.

There were three packs, and I stayed in the middle pack, not too close to avoid drafting, but I knew that I needed to keep up a good pace. The first sixty miles were mostly flat, and if I wanted to have a chance to make the twelve-hour cutoff, I had to go fast on the flats. I started at a strong pace and kept pushing hard to make as much ground as possible before we all hit the infamous "wall," a grueling 15 percent-grade long climb. I found my pace; my body overcame the initial stiffness, and I was feeling well. I was riding against the clock, no time to rest, no time to think, no time to spare. Everything was working well, much better than expected. I was going fast and feeling strong, building confidence with each mile I left behind, until I crossed eighteen miles.

By then, the bike started to feel heavier, slower, and a bit wobbly. I tried to push harder, and it got worse. When I looked down, I saw the disheartening news. I had a flat tire and no crew to help me.

After the race started, Yon went back home to pick up Jai, Tata, and the kids, who were all still getting ready for the long day. I was not sure how long Yon would take to pick them up; the only thing I knew was that I had a flat tire and no spare wheel. I had to get that flat fixed. I stopped, and instead of changing the tube, I rolled the dice. I decided to inflate it as it was, hoping that the tire sealant that Yon had put inside the tube would work. I quickly attached the CO_2 cartridge to the micro pump, opened the tire valve, and inflated the tire. To my relief, the tire held pressure, and the sealant worked. The entire process was fast, and it took me about five minutes to be back on the bike.

I continued to ride strong, pushing hard. The fact that the sealant had worked boosted my confidence. I felt in control of the race, that my strategy of using a fast tire instead of a flat-resistant tire was the right one. Though my certainty didn't last too long.

At fifty-three miles, I got my second flat tire. It was on the same tire I had had a flat earlier that day, and it destroyed my confidence in my tire strategy. I still didn't have any idea where Yon and my crew were, so I used the same technique as before, but I couldn't trust that tire anymore. When I was ready to mount back on the bike, a crew member from another athlete's crew stopped on the side of the road and offered help. I asked her if she could find where my crew was and let them know that I needed to replace my front wheel and tire. I have no idea if she ever met my crew and gave them my message.

After another five minutes lost in the battle against the clock, I was riding again, now with less confidence in my tire strategy. My concern was growing by the minute, as I had used my last CO_2 cartridges to pump the tire, and I was approaching a long section of the course in which support vehicles were not allowed. I was approaching "The Wall." At that point, it was hard not to feel like I was going to go headfirst into that wall.

A few miles later, I saw my crew for the first time; they were stopped on the side of the road. I'd been racing for about three hours, and I'm sure they wanted to know how I was doing, if the fever was gone, if the pain and soreness from the first day were better, but there was no time to spare. I could only shout, "Change the front wheel!" I could see their eyes opening wide, and they started to scramble. It was like an electric shot hitting them. Yon pointed to the front, and they got the message. Only three miles separated us from the no-support-car-allowed section. We needed to find a place to stop and change the wheel. I kept riding; my crew passed me and stopped a few minutes ahead, ready with the spare wheel on hand.

I approached them quickly, got off my bike, and gave it to Tata and Yon. "These race tires are not holding up. I prefer going with the slow training tires that are flat resistant, otherwise I won't finish this race. Let's change the front wheel where the problems are happening, and let's observe the rear one throughout the race. We may need to swap that wheel too."

While they changed the wheels, I rushed to the bushes behind the car. After three hours of intense riding, I desperately needed a pee stop. Jai and the kids ran after me. She started to spray sunscreen on my neck, the kids tried to give me food, and all of them had a lot of questions. Pee privacy was certainly not the highlight of the race.

Once again, everything was rushed, and within less than five minutes, wheels were rolling again, just in time to face "The Wall."

The first sixty miles of the race went by quickly. Overall, I was averaging more than seventeen miles per hour and feeling great. To meet the cutoff time, I needed to average 14.3 miles per hour for the whole 171.5 miles. It started to feel doable! However, a lot would depend on how well I would manage the climbs ahead. The first one was a grueling two-and-a-half-mile climb with 15 percent grade, followed by nine miles with about 12 percent grade. Right before those climbs, there was a stop to meet the crew so we could get ready for the climb, but with the challenges I had before, I didn't want to waste more time, so for me it was just a stop and go. I only got one bottle of water, taking no food or anything with me. I needed to be as light as possible for the climbs.

The climb was brutal; my speed and cadence fell drastically, my heart rate went up, and with it certainly my endorphins and other hormones. The hill was tough, but I loved it. I felt at home. Slowly but steadily, I left the Wall behind to hit the next climb, which was less steep but also had less shade. The heat was intense and forced me to consume my only water bottle fast. I was not concerned, as I was approaching the end of the no-support-car section of the race, and soon I would be able to refill my water bottles and food supply and get going. At least that was the plan, but things did not always happen as planned.

The end of the no-support-car zone came, and there was no sign of my crew. One of the highlights of the race briefing was to make sure that the crew didn't leave the athlete alone in this section of the race because it would be extremely hot. My crew was not there, but I had no option; I had to keep pedaling, even though I had no water or food, and it was about noon in the peak of summer in British Columbia. About forty-five minutes later, I heard a car approaching from the back and thought, *Okay, finally my crew is here.* Not really. It was a white minivan, and there was no car behind it. When the car passed me, the driver opened the passenger window and yelled, "You are crushing it!" I immediately recognized him. He was crewing for Slava, a Russian athlete who was behind me. I continued to ride and started to wonder how a crew vehicle from an athlete who was behind me had passed me already, but *my* crew vehicle had not. A few minutes later, I saw the white van parked on the side of the road; he was getting ready to support his athlete. His van looked to me like an oasis in the desert, and I could not resist. I stopped and asked for a water bottle. He gave me two icy-cold bottles; they were a blessing.

With no sign of my crew, I kept riding. Over an hour later, my crew passed me. After the race, I learned that they had taken a wrong turn in the no-support-car zone and kept going. It took them a while to figure out the right way and even longer to find me. Not to mention that they had to manage bathroom stops for five people and that the mood in the crew vehicle was certainly not the best, considering the sleep deprivation everyone was going through.

The crew stopped and finally, I got some food, changed the water bottles again, and hit the halfway point of the race at a good pace.

On the stop, Gabe looked at me and said, "It exploded, Dad!"

I looked at him and asked, "What exploded, Gabe?"

Yon, who was nearby, rushed to interrupt the conversation. "Everything is fine. You crushed the Wall. Just keep going!"

I didn't have time to discuss and just followed the directions to get back on the road. After the race, I learned that Yon had changed the inner tube of the tire that had gone flat a few times, but when they went back into the car, the tire exploded, scaring everyone. He changed the tube but did not remove what was causing the flat from inside the tire.

At that time, I didn't know that. My confidence level after the climbs increased a lot, and I started to think that completing the race would be possible. What I didn't know was that the worst part was still to come.

Right after the steep climbs came a long and steady climb of about 4 percent on a busy road with a strong headwind. While everyone would talk about "The Wall," the elevation profile of the course, and the heat as the major challenges for the race, no one had mentioned the challenging wind conditions. There was a constant headwind of twenty-five miles per hour for almost thirty miles on an uphill course. The climb on the bike challenges you, but the wind annoys you. That wind really annoyed me.

It was noisy and slowed me down significantly. My average speed was dropping by the minute in those harsh conditions. I decided that it was time for some energy gels to help me pick up the pace. The gels were in my bag in the car, but I had told my crew that I was not planning on taking any gel during the race, unless it was my last resort. I needed those caffeinated gels desperately, so I'd have a chance to overcome the wind.

The next time I passed my crew, who was stopped by the side of the road to hand me my water bottles, I yelled "GU," which is a popular brand of energy gels. My wife looked at me with a confused expression, but before she could ask me anything, I was gone, as I could not waste any more time. About twenty minutes later, I passed them again, and I was ready to pick up the energy gels, but no one had a gel ready for me, so I yelled again, "GU" and kept going. My wife seemed even more confused than before. I was getting very frustrated. Why was she questioning if I should have a gel or not right now? Just give me the gel! The third time I approached them and again didn't see the gels ready. I slowed down, looked at her, and said a few more words this time. "GU, I need the gels!" Jai had an aha moment and yelled back, "On the next stop!"

Another twenty minutes later, I met them again. This time I could see plenty of gels in their hands. I got some while still riding and kept going. After the race, I learned why it took them over an hour to give me the gels. The reason is a good example of how out of sync my crew and I were. When I yelled, "GU" to my wife, she understood the Portuguese word "CU," which is the swear word for anus. Yes, I was asking for an energy gel, and my wife was trying to decipher if I was swearing at her or needed butt cream because I had been on the saddle too long. Quite the situation.

Taking the energy gel helped improve my performance, but I was still concerned with the time. I knew I was cutting it close. I remembered from the race briefing session that there was a milestone on the course that I needed to be at by 4 p.m. to have enough time to complete the overall course by 7 p.m. I could not remember where it was, nor did I know where I was. I slowed down the next time I met the crew and asked them to look at the binder, find where the milestone was, and see if we were close to it yet. At the next stop, they let me know that they'd found the information in the race binder, but they were still looking for it on Google Maps. At subsequent stops, the answer was the same: "We are searching on Google, on Maps, everywhere, but we can't find this place." I could not stop to help them, I needed to get going, but how hard could it be to find the name of a place with Google these days? Extremely hard if it was not a real place. The information in the binder said that I had to reach the "false flats" by 4 p.m. False flats are uphill sections of a road that seem to be flat due to the position of the bike or the landscape around it. My crew thought it was a city, village, or even the name of a store. I was kind of lost, and my crew, who was supposed to give me directions, was totally lost.

After more than three hours of riding in terrible winds, I needed a pee stop. I told my crew, and they found a good stopping place a few miles ahead. When I gave my bike to Yon, he looked at me and said, "The car was shaking a bit; we may be facing some wind."

With a mix of disbelief and surprise, I looked at him and said, "We may be facing some wind? The wind has been killing me for the last three hours!" He had a shocked expression on his face. I was riding with strong headwinds, and my crew was not even aware it was windy. There were a lot of opportunities for better communication between me and my crew, for sure, but there was no time to fix it, and I had to get going.

I had covered 134 miles in nine hours and fifteen minutes, and I saw my average speed drop from over 17 miles per hour on the flats to 15.5 miles per hour with the hills and then to 14.3 miles per hour with the wind. Things were not looking good, and after nine hours at an intense pace, I was getting tired, but the wind was not. About a half hour after the stop, we reached the city of Princeton, where we left the valley and went for an out-and-back climb to finish the 171.5 miles in Princeton itself. Leaving the valley felt like leaving behind a wind tunnel. I just needed to climb for 18.5 miles and come back, and I had two-and-a-half hours to do that. It seemed doable.

Just after passing the city, the wind returned, but this time it was a crosswind, blowing on my left side, not only slowing me down, but also trying to wash me off the road. What unpleasant company for a ride! After riding so much, probably due to the accumulated tiredness and stress, doing the math of what speed I needed to do or how hard I should push became extremely hard. I got confused with the elevation numbers on the GPS watch, and for some reason, I thought I was okay on time. I was not.

At the turnaround point on the last peak, I passed some volunteers who were providing support and managing people's time. One of the volunteers looked at me and yelled, "You need to drop the hammer to have a chance!"

Those words hit me hard. Just from her expression, I could tell I was not in a good situation. The math time was over. I needed to give it my all, not to think about the double marathon the day after, especially because if I didn't make it in time, there would not be a double marathon. After more than eleven hours biking in grueling conditions, unbelievably, it was time to sprint.

My heart rate jumped from the 135 bpm average of the last hour to 160 bpm. It was all or nothing. I had overcome so much. The heatstroke of the day before, the soreness and stiffness of swimming 6.2 miles and riding ninety miles in a sauna-like environment, flat tires, The Wall, and over four hours of headwind. I had earned my right to complete that race. I was determined not to fail, but my invisible enemy would not take it easy on me. The wind continued to blow strongly, and with me riding mostly downhill at a much higher speed, the wind gusts were a real threat. The bike would shake like a leaf, but I didn't have the luxury of slowing down; I had to keep pushing it.

The eighteen miles back were endless and with no break from the wind. I was seeing the time fly by. I had thirty minutes left to complete the race, twenty-nine, twenty-eight. In no time, I had only fifteen minutes. With just five minutes to go before I reached the time limit, my crew passed me. That time it was different; no one was shouting encouraging words from the windows, which were actually closed. They passed without even looking at me. I don't think anyone wanted to give me the news that I had five minutes left, but the finish line was more than five minutes away. I ignored them and decided to prove them wrong. Anything can be a source of motivation when sprinting after riding for eleven hours and fifty-five minutes.

I continued to push, even harder for the last five minutes, and the time now seemed to slow down. I was tracking the seconds, and in slow motion, the timer hit 12:00:00. There was no sign of the finish line. I slowed down to catch my breath and continued to bike down until I crossed the finish line after twelve hours and eight minutes. Game over. It was the first race I had ever done in my life that I didn't finish in time.

My wife was the first one to hug me after crossing the finish line. It was a difficult moment; we were all very emotional from the defeat. Everyone's efforts were in vain. The race was over. No Ultraman title. No world championship in Hawaii. Brad, the organizer, came to talk to me, said some encouraging words that I don't even remember, and invited me to run the 52.4 miles the next day anyhow, regardless of the title and qualification spot for Hawaii. In my mind, I just wanted to rest and fly back home. A busy life waited for me. However, there was more in play than just that race. There was a reason behind all that crazy adventure. In fact, there were many reasons.

Swimming in Okanagan Lake, home of the
Ogopogo monster – Photo by Colin Cross

Biking at Ultraman Canada – Photo by Colin Cross

Day one before the start

Clueless athlete and crew

Crew plank challenge

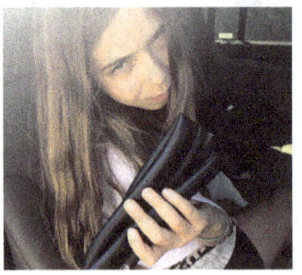

Crew tire challenge

Day two bike course and elevation charts

CHAPTER 2

FINDING WHAT MATTERS

"All the wonders you seek are within yourself."
—*Thomas Browne, English polymath and author*

2013

It was a summer day at the Riverfront area in Wilmington, Delaware, where my boss and I were working on a complex project. He stopped by my desk, and before he said a word, I could understand it all. The frustration and sadness were written on his face, and demonstrating emotions is not a strength of my Scandinavian friend. He shook his head and gave me the news that I didn't want to hear.

"Acyr, I really fought hard for you, got the support from many partners, but it was not enough. I know how much you deserve the promotion, but at this point, there is not anything else we can do; we will have to wait another year."

As Steen delivered the news, the frustration felt familiar. It wasn't just that moment, it was the many years of grinding and constantly chasing success. And for what? Something deeper had been gnawing at me, something bigger than just this promotion. I'd spent so much time focusing on work that I'd let my health slip, neglected my family, and now, with this setback, it hit me: my priorities were all wrong.

I could not change the decision or what had happened. The facts were the facts. I had no control over the decision that the company leadership had made, but I had control over how this would affect me. To put my thoughts in order I took a break, a well-deserved one.

I took two weeks off and went back to Brazil with my family to spend some time with old friends and extended family members. This time off allowed me to reflect deeply on what lessons I could take from this experience and how this would help shape my life moving forward. I considered several options, such as quitting consulting and launching a car-sharing company in Rio. I got initial traction with some investors and city officials, but searching deeply inside myself, I realized that I didn't want to settle down in Brazil. Despite the FIFA World Cup and the Olympics on the horizon, it was clear that the country was going into a recession, the political outlook was bad, and in many ways, I just didn't feel it was the moment to go back.

I took time to assess what the important things were to me. My wife, Jai, and my two kids, Sophia and Gabe, who at the time were six and one, were at the top of my priority list. Changing jobs or switching careers would not be a wise decision at that time; maybe there was more I could do with the daily work routine.

I always tried my best to be present for my family, minimizing business trips and being present at key events such as ballet rehearsals, music recitals, and parent-teacher conferences. I also helped as much as I could at home, but the long and stressful workdays (and nights) left little time and energy to do so, overloading my wife and keeping me from being fully present at home.

Not to mention, I had barely ever paid any attention to my health, and this setback could provide opportunities for me to be healthier for my family. I was significantly overweight, and I had been experiencing several issues because of that, including elevated blood pressure, high cholesterol, high triglycerides, steatosis (fat in the liver), chronic back pain, and insomnia. My health was going downhill.

When these realities confronted me, I couldn't believe the irony. I was always motivated to have a successful career, to give the best to my family, but stressed, overweight, and with health issues kicking in, I barely had the energy to enjoy quality time with my wife and kids.

Countless times, I had tried to lose weight. There were some short-term successes, such as losing about thirty pounds while living in Basel, Switzerland, right after my daughter Sophia was born. We used to live in front of the Rhine River, with a stunning view of the boardwalk and sunset over the low building and the river. That scenario inspired me, and I started to walk and jog after work, I started a diet, and my weight started to drop. It felt good. Two months later, the work picked up again, the stress level increased, and weight loss fell out of the priority list. Being healthy was just not on the list. Over the years, I had battled several health issues related to my lifestyle. The outlook was not very promising.

There were deadlines at work, but there were no deadlines to lose weight, to be healthy. I kept telling myself, *I can do it after the crisis at work is done. I don't really need to lose weight today. I can lose it tomorrow. I can resume my diet on Monday or a week from Monday.* And just like that, I stopped losing weight, and before I realized it, I gained all the weight back, including some more, of course. I could author an entire book on just about how many times this scenario repeated itself.

It was a regular cycle. A good start, some early success, and then something more important than losing weight comes into the picture, and the weight-loss program turns into a weight-*regain* program. The work was the excuse for that time in Basel, but there were vacation trips, wedding parties, Thanksgiving dinners, friends' reunions, and family gatherings. My brain somehow would always find a way to justify that I could postpone losing weight for all kinds of reasons. Sometimes, even a long road trip was an excuse to postpone the weight-loss program so I could consume sugar while driving and be more "alert."

All of that, the work, and the excuses, were all in the past now. Success at work was not guaranteed. I learned that by missing this promotion. It got me thinking. What if I shuffled the priority list a bit and put my health on top of it? With my focus, at least, I could guarantee a positive outcome for my health.

I was upset for a few days after the discussion with Steen. I considered changing my home country, job, and career, but instead, I decided to change myself. Being passed over for a promotion should not have affected me so much, but the fact was, it did. The real problem to be fixed was not where I lived, where I worked, or the missed promotion, but who I had become over time. An overworked, overstressed, and overweight person who was on track to many more health issues. In the back of my mind, I always knew I had to change and had tried many times but ended up deferring it. It was time to place my health and well-being at the top of my priority list.

What really matters

CHAPTER 3

REWIRING

"Long distance running is 90% mental,
and the other half is physical."
—*Rich Davis, American cross-country and track and field coach*

2013

The two-week break in Brazil passed by quickly, and before I could notice, I was back home. It was just a day like any other. I woke up at 6 a.m., left my home in Chadds Ford, Pennsylvania, with my wife and kids still sleeping, and drove down scenic route 52 to Wilmington, Delaware. There's nothing less exciting than a 7 a.m. project status meeting to start the day.

There I was, a bit ahead of schedule, as usual. Some critical tasks were falling behind, and things were starting to reach a point that could delay the project, so the client brought some concerns forward, and my other boss, John, promptly volunteered to take on the issues. He told the client that he could rest assured that John himself would personally take care of the issues discussed.

Right after the meeting, he pulled me aside and asked me, "Hey, Acyr, I think I'll need your help. Can we meet tomorrow at 6 a.m. to tackle some of these issues?" This was not an uncommon situation in the consulting world. Meetings were as often and urgent as needed, starting as early as 6 a.m., 5 a.m., or earlier. It was as if the urgency of client requests had a higher priority than a healthy night of sleep. In many cases, I was the one asking for the early starts. But it was different that time, and my answer was brief. "I'm sorry, I can't do it tomorrow at 6 a.m."

He was surprised, then tried to understand and find a solution. "Okay, so do you already have a 6 a.m. meeting tomorrow? We can meet before that."

I looked straight into his eyes and said, "No, I don't have a meeting. I'm going for a run tomorrow at 6 a.m." I could see his jaw drop in disbelief. For a moment, he was speechless. I understood his confusion, so I explained, "If it was a doctor's appointment, no one would be surprised; they would understand. I'm just doing what I can to avoid that appointment." I smiled politely.

After a decade in the consulting business, I had finally put my health first and communicated it to people around me in a straightforward way, drawing a line in the sand.

I had not been an active person before, so I was unsure if the surprised look on my boss's face was because I had prioritized running instead of a meeting with him or because I was actually running. It didn't matter, or at least it didn't matter *anymore*. I had decided to have a healthy life.

It was a different idea when compared to the goal of just losing weight. I could feel in my bones that this was something that could not be postponed to the next day or to Monday. A healthy life had started the moment I decided to do it, and it felt great. I have had passionate and heated discussions with my bosses before. They were not uncommon, but this time it was different; it was not about work or winning an argument to prove I was right. It was about something much more important: my health.

My boss, seeing that I was fully committed to running, backed down and, after taking a second look at his calendar, found a different slot for us to meet at a more reasonable time. I could see his emotions changing. At first, he was surprised and frustrated, but then his voice started to soften. He started to look down, avoiding eye contact with me. I was not sure if he was just too upset with me and was trying to control himself or if he was embarrassed.

After we settled on a time to meet, he almost whispered, "Do you know, you are right. We all need to prioritize our health once in a while. I really need to do the same."

I nodded and left the room, running for my next meeting that day. I never asked him, but knowing how much he worked, I'm sure his thoughts had turned to his own struggles to find the right balance among work, family, and health. It felt like he was looking for the strength to make a similar decision.

For me, the desire to be healthy for my family, combined with the frustration with my career, gave me that strength. Looking back, I can see how I channeled negative feelings and emotions to do something positive for my life. I had created space for my personal life. Not only that, but with this motivation to change, I made another big decision that I knew would be paramount to my lifestyle change.

As I started prioritizing my health, I realized I needed more than just a diet or a few workouts. I needed a challenge, something that would push me, something to aim for. Running had always seemed impossible, yet alluring. And then it hit me—what if I aimed for a marathon? It wasn't just about losing weight anymore; it was about proving to myself that I could accomplish something I'd never imagined possible.

I wanted to focus on the positive instead of the negative. The negative was my undesirable weight, and the positive was something I had always wanted to achieve, a goal. I'd always wanted to run a marathon. I thought this way, things would flow better.

I had never met an overweight marathoner; losing weight would just be a natural consequence of my positive goal. It may not seem like a big difference, but my decision to start running, this time, was not to lose weight. Instead, it was to run a marathon, a goal that inspired me. Every time I thought, and still think, of running a marathon, I feel proud of myself for daring to take on such a challenge. I got motivated by the goal. It was exciting to talk and read about it. No one should go from a sedentary life to running a marathon right away; a person needs to build up their fitness to get there, and in this process, I believed I could shave off the extra pounds.

I didn't spend much time researching or planning it. Once I decided that I would become a marathoner, it was time to get moving. I had decided to run at 5:30 a.m. the next morning, which sounded like a good plan, but the discussion with John changed my plans a bit. His initial judgmental reaction made me realize that managing running and work could be more difficult than I thought. I was beginning to think that life would inevitably get in the way, and his message in the end, that "We all have to prioritize our health once in a while," was not very encouraging either.

He was not happy and cheerful that I had decided to take my health seriously. It was more a message from someone who didn't have much time to take care of his own health and was just waiting for me to get over my midlife crisis and to give up on mine too. He probably saw it just like another attempt by an overworked person to be healthy, one that would fail in a couple of days or weeks. Being guilty of trying so many times, I could not blame him.

A lot of thoughts crossed my mind driving back home that evening, a lot of doubts and insecurities, but I was certain of one thing. I was not going to wait for the next morning to start running.

When I arrived home, Jai was with the kids in the living room, but right before that, there were the stairs to the second floor, where the bedrooms were. Instead of going to the living room as usual, I said hi quickly and rushed up to my room. I really needed to go out for a run that evening, and it needed to be before anything else got in the way. Without overthinking, I got a pair of shorts that I used for playing tennis, a plain white T-shirt, an ordinary pair of socks, and an old pair of sneakers. I was ready. I came down the stairs, and my wife was surprised to see me ready to run, but unlike my boss, she was happily surprised. While I was tying my shoes, she said, "I thought you were planning to run in the mornings, before work. Did something change?"

My answer at that time was short and shallow. "Yeah, but I just decided to run now instead." A better answer would have been something like, "I'm actually going to run now to make sure nothing changes my plan to live a healthier life." She nodded and said a few encouraging words, holding Gabe, who was one year old, and Sophia, who was six years old, close to her.

Sophia and Jai started to cheer me, "Go, Dad! Go, Dad!" as I walked out the door for my first run. It is hard to say what made me take on the bold goal of running a marathon. It could have been my aspiration to be a good example at home, the lovely support from my wife and kids, or just the desire to prove my boss wrong. Probably all of them played a role on that late August afternoon.

Stepping outside my home to go out for a run felt strange. I didn't know where to go. For some time, I felt lost. I didn't have a course in mind or place that I wanted to reach, nor was there a wild bear chasing me, so why run? Where should I run to? Before I could figure out any of these answers, I started to feel the heat. I was sweating before I even started running. It was just after 6 p.m. How was I only feeling the heat then? The answer was as simple as it was sad.

That was the first time I'd been outside that day. If not for my impulse to go running that day, I would not have even noticed the temperature. The indoor routine of *home to car to work to car to home* had become the norm without me even noticing it. For a moment, I thought that running in the morning would be a wiser decision. There would be cooler air, a rested body, a fresh mind, but the shame of going back home without running was too big to face. After a lot of hesitation, I pushed *start* on the running app button. It was time to move!

I started running without a planned route and picked three miles as the goal without much science. It just felt right for a first run. I lived in a nice townhome community that had a lot of green areas, but there were no running trails or paths. It had a small pond, and I improvised a short course, running partially on the road and partially in the parking lots by the little pond. It was a bit hilly, with many more geese than I wanted, but the area was nice.

We lived behind a winery. It had some streetlights to run at night, and more important, it was just outside my door. A loop on the improvised course was a little over half a mile, so I had to do about five loops to meet my initial goal. The first loop went well, but then each loop started to get harder and more painful than the previous one. My pace started to slow down. On the third loop, I started to walk up the small hills but continued to run after that. I also started to sweat a lot. It was so hot, or at least, it felt extremely hot but I didn't want to stop. I wanted to finish the three miles I'd set out to do, even though three miles was a long distance for someone who was living a sedentary life.

Things got painful. I started feeling my knees and ankles; the small hills seemed to get higher and steeper with each loop, but my hesitation to start turned into determination to finish. During the fifth and last lap, I started to feel better. Just the prospect that I could finish the three miles somehow made me run easier. Then, without thinking too much, I told to myself, *I'll finish this loop, complete the three miles, then I'll continue running until my home*, which was probably three hundred yards from where I expected to finish.

I'm not sure where my mind was when I had that thought, but it didn't take me long to regret it. Right after the app announced the three-mile mark, my drive winded down, and the additional three hundred yards that I once thought would be a nice sprint home to celebrate my first run turned into a drag. My body was asking me to stop, and my mind was battling with the sense of accomplishment of having completed the three miles and the newly created onus to have to run home. I was exhausted, and before having to decide on which self-imposed arbitrary goal was the right one for me to follow, I unexpectedly heard someone calling my name, "Acyr … Acyr!"

The familiar accent from my hometown, Rio de Janeiro, was hard to miss; it could only be my neighbor Dani, who was picking up his daughter, Bella, at the childcare facility nearby. My fellow Brazilian friend looked at me and, with a confused and concerned look, asked me, "What are you doing? Are you okay?" My face was bloody red, and I was so sweaty that Dani may have thought that I'd gone for a swim with the geese in the pond. I was exhausted, and meeting Dani helped me quickly decide which self-imposed arbitrary goal I needed to follow. Running was over for that day. I had planned to run three miles, and I had done so, end of story.

I stopped running, leaned on his car to catch my breath, and after a few seconds, maybe minutes, I told him that I had decided to "start running." Saying those words felt incomplete. I could imagine his thoughts. *"Good for you, Acyr. You need to lose weight. This may help you if you can sustain it."* Before Dani could comment on it, I added, "I'm going to exercise every day. I'm training for a marathon next year!" It was the first time I was telling someone that I was going to run a marathon. Anyone who knew me knew it was an audacious and nearly irresponsible goal, but I just loved how I felt saying that. It was extremely satisfying.

Dani's puzzled and concerned face changed instantly, his eyes opened, and with excitement, he replied, "Oh, that sounds interesting. I have been wanting to do something like this myself. Can I join you?"

I was shocked. I let Dani know that I would be happy to train with him and that we could pick a marathon race together, as I had not picked one yet. He then asked me the most obvious question of all. "So, what is the training plan?"

After choking a bit, I said, "Look, my sister Tata runs. I talked to her and got some insights. She recommended an app to track the runs, and I'm planning to do the short runs during the week and the long ones on the weekend, increasing the distance week by week, but there is still a lot that I have to figure out." When I finished speaking, I thought, *Now is when I lose my recently joined running partner*, but not really.

Dani looked back at me and said, "Sounds good to me! I'm going to be out of town for a while, but when I'm back, we will train together!" Dani was in much better shape than I was, so the fact that I had a head start on the training was not a bad idea. I knew I had a lot of catching up to do before I could really run with him. More than my neighbor, Dani had became my closest friend since I'd moved to Pennsylvania the year before. Our wives were close, our daughters were always having sleepovers, we went to the same gym, and our families had celebrated holidays together many times. There could not be a better partner for the crazy journey I was undertaking.

More than the partnership for training, the huge support Dani had just given to my crazy plan by asking to join made me believe that the plan may not be that crazy after all, or, in the worst-case scenario, I would not be the only person following a crazy plan! Dani offered me a ride home, but I politely declined. First, I didn't want him to have to detail clean his car afterward. Second, I needed a little time alone to let the success sink in of completing the first three miles and the fact that now I had gained a training partner. Life was about to change—a lot.

With the run completed in the evening, I arrived at work earlier the next day and, of course, surprised my boss, who, in a sarcastic voice, asked me, "So, no running this morning, sir?"

I happily answered him. "Not this morning. I decided to run last night, and running back-to-back days may be a bit too much right now.

So, do you want my help with the issues, or do you have all of them figured out by now?" We both smiled and got down to work. For my plan to be sustainable, I could not drop my work obligations. There were limits that I could not cross. I didn't have to choose between work or exercise. The answer was clear: both were important. I had to find the right balance between them. The same was true at home. There was no such thing as family or exercise. It was family *and* exercise *and* work.

The day after my first run, I decided to run again to build momentum, but that evening, my wife had an eye exam appointment, so I took Sophia and Gabe to the YMCA in Kennett Square, where I could run on the treadmill while they played at the child center. The gym closed at 10 p.m., and we arrived around 8:30 p.m., allowing plenty of time for dropping off the kids, running, showering, and picking up the kids afterward. To my surprise, the child center closed at 9 p.m.

Sophia always loved child centers; she was excited with that, but Gabe was a different story. The drop-offs were always hard and often included tears. I could not complain too much. Dropping him off reminded me a lot of my drop-offs. I never made it easy for my mom either. For a moment, I hesitated. *Should I go through this painful drop-off just to have a few minutes on a treadmill to then rush back home to get the kids ready to go to bed?* I didn't need to make up excuses; they were there, ready for me to choose. Should I just tell myself *I tried, but I can't take the blame for the child center closing before the gym closes, not allowing me enough time to exercise?* Or *My wife had an eye exam appointment; she takes care of the kids every night. Just this night, it is okay for me to skip the workout and put them to bed?* Or *I just ran three miles yesterday. It is probably a clever idea to rest to let my body recover.*

I paused and took a deep breath. With Gabe in one hand and holding Sophia's hand with the other, I decided to charge forward, face the parent guilt of a hard drop-off, and get the most out of the training I could get. As expected, Gabe started complaining the second we opened the child center door, but before things got too difficult, Sophia stepped in.

"Don't worry, Dad, I'll play with him tonight." Instead of going to play with friends her age, she got a baby toy and started to entertain Gabe. It was enough for me to step outside, change, and get a full nineteen-minute workout in. I was able to complete a mere 1.8 miles on the treadmill. But it was worth it.

Running 1.8 miles is not a remarkable distance and will certainly not affect one's fitness or weight, but I felt it was important for me to build a sequence of workouts. I needed to create momentum. Leaving the Y that night with the sense that I got the maximum I could from my training was an accomplishment. I was happy and excited that I did that run. Had I gone back home that night with the disappointed feeling that I could not run because the child center was closing too soon, it would certainly not have helped me create the momentum I needed. In addition, Sophia's willingness to entertain Gabe instead of playing with her friends just to help me exercise was encouraging, and without her noticing, she was not only an inspiration for me to be healthy but was also part of the support network that included my wife Jai and my friend Dani. More important than the exercise accomplished that night or how I felt about Sophia's support, I was starting to teach the unconscious side of my brain that I was in it for real, that there was no way out. I was ready to overcome any possible excuse to exercise, and trust me, my brain was great at finding excuses: long, stressful days at work, house chores, social events, and travels, to name a few. I had the two most important things to be successful in my quest, and it was not a detailed plan or an experienced coach. I had a loyal and close support network and the right mindset to do it. To this day, a common question that I get asked is, "How many hours do you train a week?" My answer was, and still is, "I don't know. I train as much as I can."

After running two days in a row, I got tempted to rest on the third day. Once again, the excuses were there, ready for me to pick the one I liked the most. *After two days of running, everyone needs a break*, or *Don't start too strong, you don't want to get injured.* Deep inside, I knew the 1.8-mile rushed run on the treadmill could not really be counted as a training day. I was feeling well and didn't need to rest. When I arrived home, the couch was tempting, but something else was even more tempting. *Could I run three days in a row?* I had never been able to do that, and now the opportunity presented itself. I could not pass it up. I had to go out there and run. Again.

Going out for a run straight from my front door didn't feel that strange anymore. Now I knew where to go, and I had a target, the same target from the first day, three miles. Without thinking too much, I moved to the small course near my house. I did a figure 8, going up the hill, coming down the other side, close to the pond, deviating from dozens of geese that were close to the pond, and arriving at the parking lot. From there, I continued to go down, running close to the boundaries of the parking lot all the way to the bottom of the hill, then came around, did its perimeter, and finished the loop at the center of the figure 8, close to where I had met Dani earlier that week.

There was nothing fancy about the course, but it was quiet, and having a set course that I just needed to follow somehow made it easier on my mind. It was one less thing to think about, one less decision to make. The plan that day was to run three miles. I just needed to do five laps on the course, simple and easy, and that's exactly what I did that evening. I did not need to walk the hills, and even though I was running for the third day in a row, it felt much better than the first two days.

The week passed in the blink of an eye, and before I realized, it was Friday. I decided to rest to have fresh legs for the weekend. It was time to start working on the distance.

I woke up early on Saturday, anxious about doing my first long run. One of the pieces of advice I had gotten from Tata, my sister, was not to

go too long too quickly. I should let my body adjust to the new long distance, recover, and then go longer. Her recommendation was to increase
by about 10 to 20 percent each weekend.

The challenge was that I had not done a long run yet, and going 10
percent longer on a three-mile run meant nothing. It was a rounding
error. So, I decided to give myself two weeks to get to six miles, split the
difference, rounded up, and decided that on the first long run, I would
do five miles, and on the second weekend, I would do six miles.

Once again, I started running from home, went to the goose pond
course, and started to do my laps. On the first lap, I decided to explore a
different part of the trail behind the pond that led me to the winery and
then to the main road. I decided to give it a shot and started running on
the shoulder of the road. It was a mixed experience. The cars and trucks
driving at high speed were unsettling, and I didn't feel safe. The other
issue was, of course, that the road shoulder was a collection of screws,
bolts, and auto parts that drop from vehicles and are pushed to the side
by the tires or the air of the vehicles passing by. In other words, it felt like
running in a junkyard.

On the positive side, as I was doing an out-and-back run instead
of the loops, my mind would somehow give me "satisfaction credits"
twice for the distance I had run. After running a mile going out on the
road, I'd feel as if I had run two miles, just because I had to run back
on the same course. When doing loops, you can always decide to stop
before starting a new loop, but on an out-and-back run, this option
doesn't exist.

When I arrived back at the goose pond course, I had completed
almost four miles. I didn't even see the time pass by, and when I did the
math, I just needed two easy laps on the quiet and familiar course. It didn't
sound bad at all. The small hills of the course didn't seem as challenging
as they did at the beginning of the week. My legs were feeling strong, but
something started to bother me: my knees, both of them.

I didn't stop, pushed through, and after almost one hour, I com-pleted the first long run of my quest, five miles. I finished with some mixed emotions, happy to have achieved the distance goal but concerned with the pain in my knees. A lot of thoughts crossed my mind, my con-fidence dropped, and the main question I had was, *Can I really become a runner?* By the end of this run, I was not sure.

On Sunday, I was planning to rest, to recover from the five miles, but I could not resist. I had to put my knees to the test. I didn't want to let the questions and concerns grow. If I had an issue, I wanted to know sooner than later. Twenty-four hours after my first long run, I went running. Again. At that time, I aimed for three miles on the now well-known goose pond course. My legs were tired, I was tired, it was hot, and the run was much harder than I thought it would be. My pace was slower than my first run. I dragged myself but completed the planned three miles. The knee pain was not strong, which made me feel better, but I was far from relieved.

During the second week of training, I decided to run every other day instead of every day. I wanted to have some recovery time to protect my knees. The other thing I did was to move my weekday workouts to 9 p.m., instead of running right after arriving from work, so I had time to help at home and enjoy the kids before they went to bed. As I mentioned before, for running to be part of my life, I'd have to find a way to balance it with work and family.

Adding the workouts to my life meant that I had less free time, but I could start seeing then that it was making the moments more intense. I had less time with my family in the evening, but I started to feel more present when I was with them, more aware and engaged, and the quality of the interactions increased significantly. Talking to them and getting their support to train was important. My wife and kids already expected me to go and work out in the evening, and the house started to function around this. Skipping a workout would not only affect me, it would also disappoint the whole family. I didn't want to let them down.

Dani was out of town and was planning to join me in a few weeks. I knew I had to get in better shape to have a chance to keep up with my friend. During that week, I trained on Tuesday and Thursday, and as I was starting the workout at 9 p.m., I had to leave the pond track behind and started to run on the treadmill at the YMCA. The week was also time for shoe shopping. After mentioning to Tata that I felt my knee in the long run, she recommended changing shoes, and I decided to go with the same brand and model she was used to.

I was really looking forward to my second long run; it would be my first 10k (6.2 miles), and I was going with new shoes, as recommended by Tata. It would be helpful in keeping my knee pain at bay. I woke up early on Saturday and left before the family was awake. I started right from my door and went to the well-known goose pond track. This time, I decided to stay there, doing ten laps on my figure 8 made-up course, just me. And the geese, of course!

I started at a decent pace, nothing too fast, but okay. At around three miles, things got harder. The next mile was slow and hard. I thought of quitting a few times but kept going, dragging myself. At around 4.5 miles, things started to get better. The feeling that I was close to the five miles I had done the weekend before was reinvigorating, and after crossing the five miles I started to feel as fresh as I had just started. My pace accelerated naturally, and I completed the 10k (6.2 miles) feeling great. And the best part? There was no knee pain at all.

With all the exercise, my sleep quality increased significantly, my days got more productive, the time with my wife and kids got much more fun, and my workouts became more engaging. I was also able to maintain a good weight-loss momentum. Every time I'd tried to lose weight many times before, and every time I was successful, it was temporary. The pounds would come back again shortly after, and many times, I regained more than I'd lost. Losing weight is not an easy task, and not by chance, the World Health Society lists obesity as the number one cause of disease in the world.

Jai always kept a balanced, healthy diet and made sure to pass it on to Sophia and Gabe, but that was not the case for me, especially when stress levels at work were high. The effects were immediate. She had supported me several times in trying to get to a balanced diet, but I was never successful. This time, things were different. For some reason, the more often I worked out, and the longer the workout was, the easier it became to manage my nutrition. I naturally started to crave more salads, fruits, and healthy foods in general. The sugar cravings at the beginning disappeared. Alcohol was the other thing that I crossed off my menu. I just didn't want anything to do with it. For some reason, with all the activities I was doing, I lost interest in it. I was not a big consumer of alcohol to begin with, but when the level of exercise increased significantly, my body just rejected it. I started to dislike the taste of alcoholic beverages such as wine and beer, not to mention hard liquor. The last thing I did was to replace my snacking habit by drinking hot green tea and peppermint tea. The ritual of preparing the tea, waiting for it to cool down, and savoring it without any type of sweetener became part of my day. I used to snack a lot at work. Instead, I started to drink a lot of tea.

Changing eating habits is not easy. I personally had tried countless times before and failed, but this time, things were different. My mind was different. I had a real plan and focused on running a marathon; it was something exciting. The beginning of the process of adjusting my diet was hard. I had to fight my desire to eat unhealthy junk foods: pizzas, burgers, snacks, granola bars, cereals, chocolate, candies—you name it. The detox period required a lot of willpower, but the marathon goal made it possible, and the workouts somehow made the process less painful and also accelerated it. The first two weeks were a battle against myself. After that, my body adjusted, my tastes changed, and my cravings changed. The salad greens became crunchier, the fish juicier, and each different spice more interesting. Not to mention the incredible flavor fruits started to have. I could feel the different flavor of each strawberry in a box or of the different chunks of pineapple. Eating became way more engaging and interesting, but sustaining my new eating habits required even more willpower because it was not a battle against myself but with everyone else, and the attacks came in many different forms all the time.

"Today is his birthday. I can't believe you will not eat a slice of cake!"

"We have a lunch meeting, and I already ordered pizza for everyone."

"On weekends, it is okay to take it easy and eat 'normal' food."

"Oh, you look great now. You earned the right to eat this sweet."

"I can't trust people who don't drink alcohol."

"I can't believe you will not eat chocolate on Easter."

"I can't believe you will not eat candy on Halloween."

"What matters is what you eat between New Year's and Christmas, not between Christmas and New Year's."

Being guilty myself of saying similar phrases in the past, I understand where most people are coming from. They just wanted me to have an enjoyable time without feeling guilty for breaking my diet. In their mind, as it was in my mind before, I could resume the diet after that "isolated" event. The truth is quite different. First, there are several isolated events every month. Birthdays, celebrations, holidays; there is something almost every week if you stop and think. Second, if you break your eating habits for one dinner, you may need to go back to the detox phase and have to suffer through it all over again for days or weeks to get back on a good healthy eating pattern. I was feeling so happy with my new eating and workout habits that I just didn't want to risk breaking it at all, and I learned to deflect those "attacks." Over time, they diminished, and things got easier to manage.

My workout routine and healthy eating habits were growing stronger by the day, and I was building up momentum, but I knew I needed to change the pathways in my mind for them to be sustainable. Instead of associating running with weight loss or being fat, I associated it with a big goal: running a marathon. Instead of complaining about having to work out at 9 p.m., I'd enjoy having the gym or the road just for myself; it was peaceful. Instead of feeling guilty about being away from my family while training, the pride in Sophia's eyes wishing me a good run and the happiness in Jai's voice every time I completed a workout would fuel my will to continue. There was still a long road ahead to make running a habit, but I was off to a strong start.

The start

CHAPTER 4

GOING FAR

"If you want to go fast, go alone.
If you want to go far, go together."
—*African proverb*

2013

The first two weeks of running felt great. After finishing the first 10k (6.2 miles), I could not resist going for a back-to-back run. It was awesome. I completed a three-mile run, once again on the goose pond track. I had completed 9.2 miles in a weekend, my longest distance ever, and the best part—without any knee pain. Of course, I could feel the run of the day before. I was tired; my legs were heavier, but it was well worth it. I started to see the progress in my fitness level. Maybe I'd have a chance at keeping up with Dani when we started running together. During the week, I did three short runs, between three and four miles each, completing my running preseason.

After three weeks of training consistently, Dani reached out. He was back and ready to start training together. I mentioned to him that I was using an improvised track by the pond for running, but Dani didn't show much appetite for running on goose territory. He quickly suggested that we check out the running track at the Unionville High School, which was nearby. I had never run on a track before, and in fact, I had never even stepped onto a track in my life. It sounded so interesting, so professional. I didn't need to think twice and accepted his suggestion in a heartbeat.

On Sunday morning, I picked him up at his house, and we drove to the track together, discussing the plan. I landed on a 15k (9.3-mile) target; after running the distance over two days, I now wanted to do it in a single day. Dani was a bit unsure of his target; he had not run in a while, so he would play it by ear, but it would be hard to believe that he would want to run an inch less than I would.

Arriving there, I was amazed at the sports infrastructure at the school, a public school. The track was perfect. It looked new. It was made with a rubberized material that had a great grip and was somewhat bouncy. We did some stretches, put our water bottles and jackets on the bench on the side of the track, and took off together, running counterclockwise on the track. The first laps were great. We were both fresh, talkative, and probably a bit faster than we should be, as usual. After the first three miles, it became hard for me to keep up with Dani's pace. I thought the fact that he was running in the inside track was helping him, so after he opened up about half a lap in front of me, I moved to his lane so I could catch up to him. It didn't help me at all; the track was not the one to blame.

Dani continued to leave me further behind with each lap, until he was able to lap me. We would run together for a while, then he would take off again. I'm not sure how many times he did that, but at a certain point, when we were about five miles into the run, Dani asked me, "When are you planning to stop?"

The laps were getting repetitive and harder; my legs were getting heavier, and I had started too fast to keep up with Dani as we went on. At that point, I was unsure if I could even complete the same 6.2 miles I had done the weekend before. I looked at him, and my unequivocal answer was, "I'm fine. Once I hit 9.3 miles, I'll stop." Now I had no option.

A lap at a time, I forced myself to complete the 6.2 miles; about that time, Dani stopped. He was done and decided to go for stretches. The temptation to stop was huge, but somehow, after completing the 6.2 miles, different thoughts started to play inside my mind. *Up to now, you were only catching up on what you had done last weekend. Every additional step is the new longest run you have done.* Suddenly, the 9.3-mile goal disappeared. It was not near or far. It was just not present in my mind. My goal was just to go a step more; with every step, I was beating my longest run thus far, and each step felt good. My legs started to feel lighter. The painful run gave way to a rewarding feeling that got me going. I reached seven miles, eight miles, and before I realized it, my phone indicated 9.3 miles. It was extremely satisfying.

I stopped, walked another lap to cool down, then stopped by Dani, who was patiently waiting for me. The three-week head start didn't help me go faster than Dani but it helped me go longer. After some quick stretches, it was time for our first-ever running selfie together, then time to get back home. Our wives and kids were waiting for us! Reaching 9.3 miles was a big milestone, mentally and physically, requiring more time to rest before running again.

First run with Dani

For some reason, the rest days in between the runs didn't feel right.

I was getting fitter. I felt great on the days I was exercising and not so great on the rest days. I wanted to move. Running back-to-back non-stop was a recipe for an injury, so I decided to try swimming. It was a low-impact sport that worked mostly the upper body, while running was a high-impact sport that worked mostly the lower body. It just felt like the natural choice. I mentioned it to Dani, and he was on board. We were both members at the YMCA in Kennett Square, which had a nice indoor pool that we could use to swim at night.

Going back to the pool for a lap swim reminded me how much I loved being in the water, and the exercise without impact felt good. Swimming felt like a way to clean my body and my mind. While swimming, my mind quickly goes to a different place. More than a physical exercise, swimming works as a great exercise for the mind. I'm not sure the competitive swimmer who does hard drills all day long with a coach yelling at him from the deck feels the same way, but that was not at all what I was doing. I am not the fastest swimmer, but I can swim at a decent pace forever. In my case, over there, *forever* ended at 10 p.m., when the Y closed, so the earlier I could arrive at the Y, the more I could swim.

The first three weeks of preparation were going well, but nothing compared to when I introduced swimming into the mix. Alternating running and swimming made my fitness level improve by the day, as it was my motivation to train. I started to work out every day, and it felt good. The plan was set.

- Run - further than we did the week before.

- Swim - as much as we could before the pool closed.

- Repeat.

Dani started to join more often for running and for the swimming sessions. It was a huge boost to my already high motivation. There were days when I would arrive late and exhausted from work, just to get his message: "Swimming?". There was only one right answer, independent of how I was feeling. I can't remember a single day that I didn't feel great after a swimming or running workout. We didn't have a set schedule for the week; we normally decided what workout we would do the night before, and sometimes we even changed what the workout would be during the day, due to unforeseen circumstances at work or home.

For me, the main goal was to make sure I worked out every day during the week and one day on the weekend, leaving the other weekend day to recover. To my surprise, at that time, working out every day was much easier than working out just a few times during the week. Working out became part of my daily routine.

On a typical day, I would wake up at 6 a.m., be at work at 7 a.m., be back home around 7 p.m., and have dinner with the family. While Sophia, who was six, was taking her shower, I would get ready for my workout, and Jai would get Gabe, who was one, ready for bedtime. Once I was ready, I would help Sophia get ready, brush her teeth, and put her to bed after reading *The Very Hungry Caterpillar*, *Baby Bear, Baby Bear*, or some other bedtime storybook that she loved together. She would normally take some time to decide which book she wanted, ask to read two or three books, and ask questions that required time to explain, such as, "Dad, why does the wind blow?"

After she had used all her tools to keep Dad longer, she would normally look me in the eye and say, "Good night, Dad, good luck swimming tonight. Say hi to Dani!" I would then run next door and wish good night to Gabe, who was giving way more work to my wife than Sophia was to me, give him a goodnight kiss, and leave for the workout.

I would normally leave home between 8:30 and 9 p.m., depending on how long the whole good night process would take, get in the car, pick up Dani, and go to the YMCA to run or to swim until it closed. We were often the last two people to leave the gym. After the workout, it was time to go back home, always very relaxed for a well-deserved night of sleep. Once I started exercising, my sleep quality got much better, especially after swimming.

Jai and the kids started to join Dani and me on the long runs on the weekend, and Dani's family sometimes would join us too. They would do some laps on the track and play on the field while Dani and I would run for hours around the field. One thing was clear—I was not alone on that journey.

A support network can make or break one's dreams. The support network could be centered around a gym, a running club, a personal trainer, or any online group, but for me, it had to be centered around my family. Engaging Jai and the kids in the process made the journey worth it because we could share big goals, overcome challenges together, and achieve things as a team, helping us build stronger bonds. It is not rare to hear stories of people who had to stop their plans because it was affecting the family or marriage, which suffered because one wants to go one direction and the other doesn't. For things to work for me, they had to work for them too.

Family run on the track with Dani and his family in the back

CHAPTER 5

RUNNING TO MYSELF

"Courage is contagious."

—*Brené Brown, American professor and social worker*

2013

I was twenty-one, finishing up college while doing a full-time internship program at an oil company in Rio. I shared an open area with three employees from that company, and on a random afternoon, I was head down, working on my computer, as usual, when Pete, the employee who had the desk closest to me, came back from a discussion with his supervisor. Things were different. His walk was different. He sat on his chair and looked at me and others in the same area. His eyes were watery and red. What had happened was more than obvious. He then started, "It happened. I'm not going to work with you guys anymore. I just wanted to say that I'm going to miss you all. I really liked working here, but life goes on." He then turned to me and said, "Acyr, I really like you as a person, but I have to say that I felt more lonely sitting on your side for the last few months than when I was sitting alone in the data center room. The servers talked to me more than you did. Life is not all about work."

Of course, I felt horrible for him and tried to apologize, but it was too late to make any real connection. After he left, the other people in the room told me that he was going through a challenging time in his personal life, which impacted his performance at that time and that it ended up leading to the termination. I was going through a busy time, doing the full-time internship there while finishing up engineering college. My parents had recently divorced, and the family was falling apart, as well as my dad's business. At that time, I blamed what happened on my lack of time, but the reality is, my life didn't get any slower after that. I became engaged in more demanding jobs, travel, marriage, and kids. However, somehow, after receiving his genuine feedback, I became more social. Before that, for me, work was work, period. If you need help, find a friend or a therapist for that matter. This socialization of mine became even better after I made running an ambition.

When I started to lose weight because of running, a lot of people approached me to learn what was going on, and topics relevant to exercising would invariably come up. Running became the conversation topic of a lot of the breaks. To my surprise, the running community was strong. Every day, I'd learn about someone's new experience, share experiences of my own, and create deeper connections with people I used to see every day but whose life outside work I knew little about. Running made me more approachable to people in a way. It showed the world that a workaholic like me was also human.

In one of these discussions, Sam, a friend of mine, let me know that he had just signed up for the Philadelphia Half Marathon in November and that registration was still open. It was late September, I'd been training for just four weeks, and my original plan was to do a half marathon within a year of training, but that discussion triggered my interest. My long runs were already over nine miles, and the word in the running community was that if one runs ten miles in training, he or she will be able to run a half marathon. Some of the reasons are that, for a race, one rests leading up to the race (tapering) and rests after the race (recovery).

During training, rest and recovery are limited; otherwise, it is hard to make progress with one's fitness. Not to mention that the adrenaline and enthusiasm of a race day plays a key factor too. With about four weeks left before the race, I was sure I could do that. I also had another motivation for the race. The wintry weather was quickly approaching Pennsylvania, and I thought that a short-term goal could boost my motivation to overcome the adverse weather.

I quickly scanned the race website and learned that there was also a kids' run the day before. I saw this as a wonderful opportunity to engage my family in the process. I called my wife. None of us had ever done any type of race before; we had no idea what it really meant, but she understood the motivation, liked the idea of the kids' run the day before, and was supportive. Before either of us changed our minds, I jumped on the computer and registered Sophia, who was six years old, and me for our first races. As soon as I got the confirmation email, I forwarded it to Dani with the message, "Goal 1:59." In about ten minutes, I got his reply, with his registration attached! I also shared the news with my sister Tata, who was already a runner and had provided me with a lot of support since the beginning. She got excited with the news and decided to come all the way from Brazil to join me for my first race. Training became a serious business then, from one day to the other. I got a racing team and a deadline with place and a goal: to finish the half marathon in less than two hours.

I was already committed to the training plan I had laid out, and the deadline helped me focus even more. And the best part? I was not alone. Without much planning, I built a staunch support network with Dani, Tata, and Jai. We all started to use the same running app, track each other's training sessions, and share pictures, comments, and questions. It really made things way more interesting and engaging. Before I could think too much, I had signed up for my first race and engaged my family and friends in the journey. I knew that I didn't know what I was getting myself into, but that fear of the unknown fascinates me. It engages, I get so intrigued and motivated that it is easy to motivate others, and once I motivate others, I also motivate myself!

As the Philly race turned into a family project, Jai and the kids started to join me for the long runs on the weekends at the running track at Unionville High School. I would normally go earlier with Dani to get some miles in before my wife would arrive with the kids an hour or so later, so it was not so boring for them. Sophia started to train for her half-mile kids' race, which she started to call the half marathon for kids. Her initial excitement with the race and ambitious goal to *win* the race quickly gave space to her fears when she tried to run a quarter mile for the first time. She looked at me and said, "Dad, this is too hard!" She was exhausted, and the concern was stamped on her face. Her eyes started to fill with tears when I hugged her and said, "Don't worry, it is hard for Dad too, but we will do it. We just need to practice."

For a moment, I thought she would quit, but no, she just needed to let it out a bit, get back on the track, and try again, slowly but steadily. She was always active, and she loved running around. I knew she got that, but she needed to build her confidence to do the race. Tata sent her a kids' running book as a gift, which taught some walk/run/sprint techniques and some fun running drills that helped her feel she was doing the right things to prepare for the race. It was rewarding to see her confidence building up with every weekend that we trained together. She was not the only one building up confidence; I was doing that too, and every week, I would go further than the week before, just as I had planned. I'd increase the long runs somewhere from 10 to 20 percent each weekend, building up cardio and muscles, and in the process, reducing the weight naturally.

After finishing a long run and Sophia finishing her half-mile practice, we both sat on the running track, and I took a selfie. It was a nice picture, and I posted it on Facebook, something I had not done in a while. We both looked tired but happy. Sophia wore her purple running shirt, and I wore a white one with some bright-yellow details on the sleeves that contrasted with the perfect red running track and caught people's attention. It also generated a lot of reactions. Most people liked the picture and made supportive comments, but some comments from people that I'm sure loved us and were concerned with our well-being were interesting. A good French friend, with whom I worked in Switzerland, wrote, "Acyr, what is this? At your age?" I was thirty-seven years old, but if anyone asked my age back then, the most appropriate answer would have been, *I'm ten years younger than I was six months before I started running.* My French friend was not alone. My parents, in-laws, and many other friends close to me had similar reactions, especially because the change was happening fast.

With Sophia on the running track

Speed was my major ally. Not the speed on the track, I didn't really care about that, but the speed with which change was occurring. Changing things fast avoided distractions and reduced the chances of being sidetracked. Losing weight would make me run and swim better, which would make me feel and sleep better, which would make me eat better and end up making me lose more weight. To enter this virtuous cycle is not easy; it requires a lot of willpower and effort, but once you're in it, it is incredible. You feel unstoppable. Working out is not a "chore" anymore; it is a pleasure.

As Dani and I started to ramp up the long runs over the weekend, the weight loss accelerated, and I started dropping more than five pounds a week, every week. It was just unbelievable. Hard for a change like that to go unnoticed, even for people who saw me every day at work. In the first two months, I lost over forty pounds, and I started to look quite different, which triggered several interesting reactions in people. Most people seemed happy and curious to learn more about how I was losing weight and were surprised at how much younger I looked. One of my bosses, Matt, once said, "Are you Benjamin Button or what? Every day, you look younger. In no time, you will be back to college if you continue like this!" Matt, who I used to see every day, got inspired to change his lifestyle too and, in a couple of months, lost over fifty pounds himself. He was not the only one.

Sharing my experience with the people around me was rewarding and kept my motivation going. My friends would often provide several tips and recommendations on where to find healthier foods. The sandwiches and pizzas of working lunches and dinners started to be accompanied by a special salad option, just for me. At home, Jai continued to be extremely supportive, and I even decided to follow one of her recommendations that she had insisted on for many years, which was to prepare my own food at home and take it to work. This was just something that I could never see happening a few months before. Of course, my wife teased me a lot for doing that then.

Healthier eating habits created unexpected connections with people around me, but nothing compared to the connections with the running community. Nearly every day, I would learn about a new runner in my circle of friends and coworkers, each one with their own interesting story. I received many lessons and tips about several topics, including places to run, shoe recommendations, how and when to stretch, and many more.

My life at work and outside work got much more interesting.

Crowdsourcing all the information was fun, and people's stories were inspiring. This was my personal journey, and I was following it at my own pace. I decided not to get professional support or to go deep into theoretical research. Everyone is different, but I learn best by doing, and that's what I did. I chose to learn running based on my own experiences. This made the process more interesting, but not any easier. It became far more engaging. I was eating healthier because I would exercise better, not because someone was telling me to cut certain carbs, and I was exercising because I felt great, not because I was following someone else's plan for me to lose weight. I wanted to swim after the long runs. My legs felt strong after that.

During the swims, I learned that I could not push the wall on the turns because if I did that, my calf would cramp up. I didn't want anyone telling me what to do or why I was feeling that way. I wanted to learn by myself, to experience it myself; nothing could get me more engaged in the entire process than that. Hiring a coach who would tell me what to do would certainly increase my knowledge, but it would undoubtedly reduce my motivation. A lack of knowledge or experience would not stop me, but a lack of motivation certainly would. Again, everyone is unique. Some people may prefer to join a running group or hire a coach. If that helps them, go for it.

Most people were supportive and, in a way, contributed to helping me continue on this fun and engaging journey, but, as always in life, some people's attitudes didn't contribute, even though they might have had good intentions. I vividly remember a work colleague asking every time we met each other, "Are you sick? You have been losing weight so quickly." Okay, he was joking—at least I assumed so—but his joke didn't really help. Some people would bring serious concerns with running, but of course, they were not runners. The most common one was with the knees: "Don't do that; running is bad for your knees!" followed by concerns about the heart. "I heard people may have a heart attack running marathons," not to mention the super-motivational stories that people would share about a friend who was hospitalized and almost died because they got dehydrated or about a friend who knows a person who had a heart attack while running or who tore his knee. There were countless stories like that. Normally I'd not engage too much in those discussions or try to prove I was right. I'd rather spend my energy with the people who had experience in running, to learn from their successes and failures, instead of from someone's fear.

Choosing which connection to deepen and which ones not to spend so much time with is always more art than science. In many ways, running created more connections with the people around me and made me more approachable. In the eyes of the others, it probably made me more human.

CHAPTER 6

GONNA FLY NOW

"Every champion was once a contender
who refused to give up."

—*Rocky Balboa, fictional American boxer portrayed by Sylvester Stallone*

2013

The race date was approaching quickly, and with it, the chilly weather, which was one of my main concerns. The race was the perfect short-term goal to get me engaged and motivated to continue to train as the temperature started to drop. The small daily accomplishments were also great motivators. Going a bit longer in every run, being a bit lighter every day, and before I realized it, Dani and I were running 13.1 miles already, two weeks before the actual race. My best time for that distance was two hours and one minute. I was already close to the 1:59 goal for the race, but the more time I spent training, the less worried I felt about the time.

To be able to run long distances, enjoy nature, and see myself transforming into another person was so rewarding that pace and race time really took a back seat. I started to explore different parks nearby, got to know beautiful trails, and got way more connected with the region we were living in. The time in the woods, by the creeks, and with the wildlife was great. It was recharging my motivation, confidence, and well-being. In some way, I started to feel connected with my childhood.

I grew up in Rio de Janeiro, but as a kid, I spent most of the weekends in a house in the mountains about three hours from Rio, a city called Nova Friburgo. I always loved to hike and explore the woods with my friends. There were small waterfalls, creeks, and many trees. It was as big and mysterious as the Amazon Forest, at least for the six-year-old version of me. People used to tell stories of jaguars being around, but the only animals that I remember seeing were opossums, coatis (the Brazilian version of a raccoon), armadillos, and a lot of frogs. My mom hated them. It didn't really matter. Being out in nature was fun and felt way more like home than the busy city. Running was starting to bring me back to that experience, to reconnect me with the things I enjoyed.

With each day, the training distance increased. Dani and I had to start worrying about hydration and nutrition. The cold alleviated the hydration needs, and we could easily manage it by carrying some water. For nutrition, Tata had recommended using running gels, something popular within the running community. Though they felt quite weird at first; they were pure sugar. A lot of people have GI issues when taking them in the beginning, so testing them was important. As I was still working on losing weight, I was hesitant to use them, but I broke down and used the last long runs to test some of those gels.

The immediate increase in performance was evident, especially when I took the gels with caffeine. I felt fast and unstoppable. For the record, I do not drink coffee, never did, even though I was born and raised in Brazil.

The race was a new experience, and to be better prepared for it, I decided to take a session with a running coach at the YMCA the weekend before the race. The session was good. He taught me some good running drills and stretches. He also gave me some tips on what to expect in the race, how to get water during the race, and when to have the gels. He also explained the importance of tapering (which means reducing training volume before the race), so my performance could peak on race day.

He also gave me some feedback on my running form. I remember him saying, "Pretend you have a quarter in each hand, and you are holding them with your fingertips. When you run, your arms will swing back and forth. Those quarters should rub on the side of your shorts. Your fingers should not touch your shorts, just the quarter. To run faster, just swing your arms longer and faster." It was a good session, and it helped me plan the last week of training. I had started using some running drills back then, but I never paid too much attention to the imaginary quarters. I continued to run with my hands in front of my body, with my elbows at a ninety-degree angle, as I was doing before. Running with them out to the side felt strange, so I naturally just let it go.

Tata arrived a few days before the race. She was shocked at how different I looked. We went for a short run. She tried some of the gels that would be given out during the race, and before I realized it, race weekend had arrived.

From an initial plan to do a half marathon in one year, the two and a half months just flew by. On one hand, it felt like everything had gone too fast. It was as if I blinked in September, and when I opened my eyes, it was already November, and I was in decent shape to run a half marathon. On the other hand, I felt I had learned a lot in only two and a half months, including discoveries about running shoes, gear, and nutrition. I met new people and "known" people in a new way. I discovered new places and, more important, a new self. I was strong and ready for the race. I was excited for it, but before my race, there was another one, just as important as mine. It was Sophia's first race!

When Saturday morning arrived, we drove to Philly to pick up the race package, which included the race bib to use on Sunday and a nice long-sleeved shirt with the saying, "For the love of running." By coincidence or not, I was starting my running journey in the City of Brotherly Love, running with my sister, who lived five thousand miles away, and with the brother that life gave me, Dani. Sophia also checked in for her half-mile kids' race, where she got her own bib and a nice shirt, but she didn't have much time to enjoy the kit. Her race was happening just a bit later that day. It was time to get ready!

We attached the bib to her shirt, made sure she knew the course and, most importantly, made sure she could relax beforehand. We all warmed up together. I taught her some running drills that I learned from the YMCA coach. Tata and Jai suggested additional ones, and Sophia taught us some fun drills that she had learned in her book *Running for Kids*. Gabe, who was one year old at the time, was having a blast, and we would alternate helping him imitate his big sister.

Sophia let us know that she was thinking of using the technique she had learned in the book as well, which was to alternate jogging, sprinting, and walking. We all gave her a lot of support to do so and encouraged her to have fun and not to worry about time or anything. She was excited but nervous. By following the techniques, she had learned in the book and practiced before, she was able to relieve her apprehension. It was time for Sophia to join her age group and line up for the race while the rest of us lined up to capture her experience as best we could. The course departed from the Benjamin Frankin Parkway and looped around Spring Garden Street, passing in front of the Philadelphia Art Museum and the iconic Rocky steps, to finish at the same place as they started. We would see her just at the start and finish lines.

"Ready, set, *go!*"

The kids blasted off, some probably trying to break the kids' half-mile world record, others at a more moderate pace, and a few looked for their parents to support them along the way. Sophia was in the middle group, and we could cheer her up from the start! After a few turns, the kids disappeared while following and being followed by the race coordinators. With everyone watching the kids fading, the silence took the space of the lively atmosphere at the start of the race. Not even Gabe would say a word.

Everyone's attention moved from one side of Spring Garden Street to the other, and some inevitable questions started to come to mind. *Will Sophia be okay? Will she enjoy the experience?* It is hard not to be concerned when your six-year-old is out of sight in the middle of a big city doing something she was afraid of. Time slowed down. Seconds felt like minutes.

The silence was broken only when the first kids appeared when returning from the art museum, bringing back the lively atmosphere to the supporting parents, who started to cheer and celebrate as more kids reappeared and sprinted to the finish line. Over half of the kids had arrived, and still, there was no sign of Sophia. The seconds now felt like hours, especially when Jai started looking at me with the question written on her face, *Are you sure this was a good idea?*

After a little while, a little girl with a sweaty red face appeared. The tension dissipated like magic. It was Sophia! She was working hard, and it was clear that she was determined to complete the race. We started cheering for her, and she didn't even look at us. She was focused on crossing that finish line.

The happiness oozing out of her when crossing the finish line was contagious. She was exhausted but happy with her first medal and accomplishment. She was not the only one happy with that. We all were proud of her for jumping on something completely new and, at such an early age, managing to overcome her fears. I was happy to give her the opportunity to see different things in life, to grow, and to get a taste for sports.

Growing up, I didn't have any athletic models at home. My mom never ran, cycled, or played any sports that I can remember. At most, she would do recreational walks on the beach boardwalk in Rio, and trust me, she was way more active than my dad was. If there is a word to define my memories of my dad when I was a child, that word would be "sleep." He was always sleeping. Even when he was driving. Someone would have to travel with him to make sure to keep him awake. Most times, my mom would have that job.

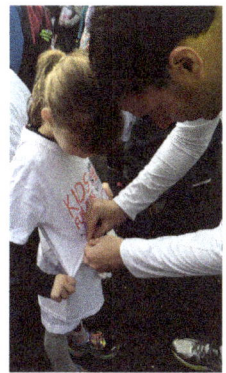

| *Preparing Sophia for her first run* | *Sophia with me and Gabe with Tata* | *Sophia's first medal* |

With Sophia's first race in the bag, it was time for us to celebrate and get ready for my first race the day after.

Race day arrived, and the day started early, not only for me but for the whole family. Jai, Tata, and I woke up around 4:30 a.m., had a short breakfast, and it was time to take the kids, while still sleeping, to the car so that they could have their final hour of sleep as we drove. Of course, we got a bit behind schedule, which was probably good to pump up my adrenaline before the race. We arrived in the city around 6:30 a.m., and it was shocking to see how many people were quickly getting together for the race. When I signed up, I had no idea how large these races could be. Philadelphia had over twenty thousand people registered for the marathon and half marathon. Later, I learned that some races have over forty thousand runners. It was mind-blowing to learn how many people love the sport, and I had been missing out on it.

After parking, we had a short walk to the starting area and began to feel the energy of the other runners, and the support from family and friends who were cheering for the runners. The first surprise was an extensive line of runners, but we could not understand the reason. Most people already had their bibs and shirts, so the lines could not be to pick up the race kit. After walking a while, we could see the start of the line and realized that these were lines for portable toilets, which were big bottlenecks in every kind of race. Athletes want to use them just moments before the start of the race, to reduce the chances of having to stop during the race, especially because everyone's hydration is high.

One of the priorities of every runner is to drink plenty of water in the days leading up to the race. This begins days and sometimes weeks before the race, allowing the body to absorb as much liquid and minerals as possible so one can start the race on top of his or her hydration level. As a side effect, people need to go to the restroom more often than normal. If you add the pre-race adrenaline, you can understand why so many people were in line. Things were not different for me, and that idea of a quick stop in the restroom before the race proved to be harder than anticipated. I walked back to the end of the line, with the race start time approaching and the bathroom line moving, of course, at a slower pace than anyone wanted. The adrenaline was getting higher and higher.

After about ten minutes (which seemed like an hour to me), it was time to kiss Jai and the kids and join Dani and Tata in the corral for our tentative half marathon time, 1:59.

The starting line was a mix of some people chatting while others were just concentrating on the challenge ahead. I was in the second group. When a big challenge lies ahead, my mind takes the steering wheel, not my mouth. I love the fact that I can just switch off all the noise around me and only focus on what I believe is important to overcome that challenge. Despite all the conversations in that starting line, for me, it was a deep silence, only broken at 7 a.m. by the gun signal that the race had officially started.

The elite athletes took off, followed by the first waves of age-group athletes, divided into groups based on each one's tentative completion time. The goal of dividing the racers into groups is to minimize traffic during the race, so a faster athlete doesn't have to deviate from slower ones. This approach works but has its limitations, as the racer enters the tentative completion time without any validation of former race times or training times, so people tend to be optimistic about their planned finish time.

The groups were in sequence, like waves, creating a nice flow of people moving in an orchestrated way. In no time, it was time for our group to move. First, a slow walk, and as we were getting closer to the starting line, the walk started to pick up; and as Dani, Tata, and I crossed the starting line, running started. The race had officially begun for us! We quickly passed Jai, Sol, and Gabe. I high-fived them and went off to my first race ever, together with my team and an ambitious goal at that time: 1:59. Why 1:59? No science behind it. It just sounded much nicer than 2:00.

After passing the starting line, all the stress, concerns, and fears were left behind. No more worries with the preparation, with the parking lot, bathroom lines, food, etc. It was time to enjoy it, and I felt great. I'm sure the wave start helped, but it was still packed, and the overall pace in the beginning was not great. Dani, Tata, and I would look at each other, and without a word, we could understand what we were all thinking: *When will this clear up?* The course ran through downtown Philly, with a lot of turns at the beginning, which made things even harder. It was packed! To avoid walking, we had to go to the outside-most possible in each turn, turning it into a harder and, eventually, longer course. Things were getting frustrating.

After a few minutes, I decided not to wait for it to clear and started to zigzag the course to pass the slower runners in the front. Dani got the message and came right after me. Tata was more concerned with finishing it than she was with time, especially after the long flight from Brazil. She was there for fun and to support me, not to beat any personal record. The zigzag started to work, and despite it making the course longer and harder, we could at least run at the pace we were planning for. Sometimes, I would get stuck behind some people, and Dani would open up another way in the middle of the crowd, and I would start to follow him till he got stuck, and I would open a new way.

This zigzag between the slow runners and the back-and-forth between Dani and me went on for over an hour during the race. It was extremely frustrating. I didn't see that coming; I could never have thought that people would just register unrealistic tentative finish times just to be in faster groups. Facing so many runners who were slower than me in a race caught me off guard, but I was not ready to give up on my goal, so there we went, for over an hour, squeezing ourselves between runners, jumping on the sidewalk and back where there was space to overtake someone. Dani and I continued to push hard, and when things cleared up, Dani increased the pace. I was feeling a bit tired. All the dodging took some of my energy, so I decided not to keep up with Dani and instead to do my own race, at my own pace. I took a running gel and picked up the pace a bit. I was still determined to complete it in less than two hours.

The race was a mix of a sports event and a street party. On every corner, there was a surprise, people singing and listening to loud music. There were a lot of signs and messages for the runners, as well as people dressed in costumes. Sometimes, it reminded me of a street carnival. At around eight miles, the hardest part came: a hill that, at the time, seemed like a huge mountain. I remember my struggle to keep the pace uphill. I worked hard but started to feel that the two-hour goal would slip through my fingers. After a few hard miles, I started to see the top of the hill, and I could clearly feel the difference in my body. The excitement of reaching the top was giving me an extra dose of hormones that recharged me for the last two miles of the race. During the downhill, I let it all out. I knew the only chance to make the 1:59 time was if I could gain some time back on the downhill, offsetting the time lost on the uphill. Runners are normally more cautious on downhills to prevent injuries, but I didn't have time to think about this. If I wanted the time, I had to take some risks.

With every stride downhill, I pushed harder, went faster, and felt stronger. In no time, I was passing everyone who had passed me during the uphill, and more. Not a single runner passed me during that downhill. I was flying, trying to recover the time lost, playing dodge-runners while climbing uphill. At the bottom of the hill was the last mile and a half. It was my home stretch, time to give everything—and I did. The last half mile was a sprint. The Rocky Balboa soundtrack playing on the streets of Philadelphia gave a nice touch to the end. I made an all-out sprint to cross the finish line in one hour and fifty-seven minutes. It was extraordinary. I high-fived Philadelphia's mayor, Michael A. Nutter, who was down at the finish line, greeting all runners individually.

Jai and the kids were there to cheer for me, as always. Everyone was delighted; it was a special moment. We hugged and kissed each other, took pictures at the finish line, and found Dani and his family to celebrate together. After a few minutes, Tata arrived at her own pace and was also happy. We all cheered for her, hugged, and celebrated together! The energy from the crowd, the finishers, the music, everything was remarkable. It made it worth the hard training and waking up so early. Being in Philly, there was no better place to celebrate than the Rocky steps at the Philadelphia Art Museum. We first took pictures with Rocky's statue, which was dressed in a race shirt, then headed to the steps. With Rocky's soundtrack playing on a loop at the nearby finish line and the tank refueled by accomplishment, it was time to run up the Rocky steps together to enjoy the iconic view of the city of Philadelphia. I could not have had a better backdrop for a big transformation, a comeback for a different life, a healthier life.

After three months of arduous work, both physical and mental, the results were starting to appear. I had failed several times in my tentative plan to live a healthy life, but I had never given up on it.

Prep before Philly Half Marathon — *Brotherly love ready to go* — *Half marathon completed*

Traditional picture at the Rocky Balboa statue — *Gabe celebrating on the Rocky steps* — *Family picture at the finish line*

CHAPTER 7

GHOSTS FROM THE PAST

"You cannot find peace by avoiding life."
—*Virginia Woolf, English author*

1980s

Growing up, I was the thin child at home, and my sister, Tata, was the chubby one. My mom would take me to swimming lessons during the week, and on the weekends, I'd spend the whole day riding bikes or hiking the trails around our country house. I'd not eat much. My mom would force me to eat. I remember when I was around eight years old, my mom would not allow me to leave the dinner table before I ate everything on my plate. My sister would stay with me at the table, and when Mom got her eyes off the two of us, I'd give all my food to Tata. She loved the rice and beans and everything else. The only thing that I remember eating were the pieces of steak and some cooked manioc flour, that was it. I would not even eat french fries; Tata would.

I'd also eat egg whites, never the yolk. They would make me feel sick. But we could not throw away the yolk. So, what we used to do was save the yolk for my sister, who would batter it with sugar. She loved it. I would almost throw up just watching her eating it. When I would go on fishing trips with my dad, my sandwiches were the "special" ones. Everyone would get a simple bread, butter, cheese, and ham. For me, I would only eat bread and ham, no butter, no cheese. I can't remember how we got there, but if it had butter or cheese, I would just not eat it, and I would be fine. My parents were not, especially my dad.

When I was around eleven years old, my dad lost his job and decided to start his own company. We faced some years of financial hardship and had to sell our car, reducing the trips to the country house significantly. I remember telling my mom that I wanted to stop swimming, which was not a hard decision for her, considering all the difficult things she was dealing with. When my dad got back on his feet, Tata started having high school classes on the weekend, and the active days of swimming during the week and biking on the weekends were gone before I realized. With a less active lifestyle and eating *more* food, not necessarily *better*, I started to put on weight, which only got worse in my teenage years, especially because of drinking.

Elementary school pictures. On the left, fourth grade (1985), on the right, fifth grade (1986).

Being a shy kid, I always lived more in my own world than in the real world. I was never social, but as a teenager, the peer pressure, the desire to be accepted and belong to a group, and the necessity to overcome shyness to ask girls out, and many other things, led me to drinking. I absolutely hated alcohol. The smell, the flavor, the feeling. But that was secondary to the desire of a fourteen-year-old to fit in with a group that was older than him. Yes, all my friends were older than I was because I skipped a year at school. It was not due to my advanced maturity or intellect but due to my sister's. Tata's teacher recommended she skip a grade, and my mom, to make sure I didn't feel bad, proposed to the school that my sister would only skip if I could also skip a year.

With no exercise, poor eating habits, and drinking as the social currency of my teenage years, my weight escalated. My sister, on the other hand, was way more self-aware than I was and decided to change the story that was written for her in her teenage years. She joined a gym, started a diet, and took control of her own health. As teenagers, we had flipped the roles at home. She was the one in good shape, and I was the chubby one, not that I saw it that way at the time.

I remember a girl at school who I was doing group work with. She said to me, "Acyr, in fourth and fifth grades, you were one of the cutest kids in class, but now you gained weight. You need to lose it." But I was in denial. I stayed in denial for a long time, getting wasted more often and avoiding the scale at all costs, which worked until I turned eighteen.

At eighteen years old, every man must enlist for the military in Brazil, and so I did. I registered for the navy, and on registration day, we had to do eye tests and several other exams. One of the steps was being weighed and a navy officer would write down the weight on the form. The situation was uncomfortable. Apparently, I didn't have a way out. I'd finally have to face my weight after many years. My luck seemed to change when a higher-ranking officer joined us in the room and asked for everyone to speed up because the line was getting too long. To gain time, the officer in charge of the scale decided to skip the scale and just ask people for their weight directly. The officer asked the guy in front of me, who replied, "Eighty kilos" (176 pounds).

The officer then looked at me and asked the same thing. Without knowing any better, I gave the same answer, "Eighty kilos." If it worked for the guy in front of me, it should work for me too. And it did. We continued all the other steps, probably a dozen of them, and in the end, an officer was reviewing the forms. When he looked at me and looked at the form, he said, "This is not right. There is no way you weigh eighty kilos. Let's double check that." My self-reported weight didn't last too long. After an endless walk, we arrived at the scale. The mystery was about to end. I stepped onto the scale—114 kilograms (251 pounds). That number hit me hard, probably the first time I understood I had put on way more weight than I thought.

It took some time to sink in. Later that year, I decided to lose weight. I joined a kickboxing gym with some friends, reduced food, and drinking, and started to step on the scale every day. The goal was set to get to 194 pounds before a monthlong trip my friends and I were planning for the summer. Mission given; mission accomplished. I reached the target weight, and the trip was memorable. By the end of summer, things were going well, but then another financial crisis hit our home.

My dad had led all the companies he had created to bankruptcy at once and with a lot of debt across the board. From one day to the next, life as I knew it disappeared. No more cars at home, no kickboxing, no money for college or the basics at home. Phone lines were cut, and even power was cut. In the middle of the storm, my dad tried to convince me to stop studying engineering and move to his farm in the middle of nowhere to manage the milk production of one of his businesses.

He argued that moving to the farm would be much better for the family because by studying engineering, I would, at most, get a poor job afterward. In his view, I would not be making more than two thousand

Brazilian reais (four hundred US dollars) per month, even ten years after graduation. When I said no, I was the weak, wimpy, stupid kid he could not count on, a coward who was not willing to do what was necessary to save the business. Oh yes, I have heard this and similar "praise" many times, but not even close to what my mom had heard and lived through.

That time was hard for her, and she had to deal with it mostly on her own, as both her parents and her only sister had passed away. Enough was enough, and after a life of being put down, she asked for a divorce. In the middle of this storm, I prioritized my studies and my career, and my weight—or health, for that matter—took a back seat. Not by surprise, my weight came back up over time. This was the first of many times that I tried to take control of my weight until something else distracted me from it, and the weight would go back up, most times higher than it was before—a sad roller coaster. There were periods in which things were bad and others when they were worse, but they were never good.

This time, things were different. Running was at the center of it. The marathon goal that was beyond any of my wildest dreams was now close. I could almost touch it. Could I finally get off that twenty-year roller coaster ride? I had been able to manage the schedule between home, work, and training, and I found a great training buddy. I had finally found a diet routine that was working for me, and I had sustained it now. It was a win that I had achieved in the process of aiming for a bigger goal—the marathon. However, a healthy lifestyle was only one of the obstacles I had to overcome. Another obstacle was running in the winter, and I had yet to work on that.

Chapter 8

Growing Pains

"If it doesn't challenge you, it doesn't change you."
—*Fred de Vito, American author*

2013

After the race in Philly, I felt awesome. It gave me a lot of confidence. The weekend after the race, Dani and I decided to go for an even longer run. Without hesitation, we agreed on an eighteen-mile training run. It was late November, and the temperature was dropping by the day, but there was no lack of motivation, especially after completing the half marathon in less than two hours.

My wife raised concerns about the weather. She was afraid it was too cold to run outside and reminded me of a case that had happened four years earlier in Minneapolis, a week after we moved to the United States. At the time, we saw on the local news two casualties that had happened because of the freezing weather, and one of them was a runner who defied the weather and went running outside. He never made it back home and died of hypothermia.

I remembered the case, but I was not inclined to let the weather dictate when I could or could not run. I heard a saying while living in Switzerland: "There is no bad weather for running, there are only bad clothes." I didn't have warm running gear at that time, but I had some ski gear that could do the job. Moreover, the winter in Philly is about the same as the one in Europe, and the saying makes sense, I don't think it is valid for the winters that I experienced while in Minnesota, though.

Early Sunday morning, Dani and I drove to the top of route 52 and agreed to run down the rolling hills to the city of Wilmington, Delaware. Here, we could find the distance we were looking for, and it would be a pleasant run.

I put on my ski fleece, ski hat, and mask but decided not to go with the ski gloves, as they were too bulky to run in, so I decided to use a light running glove that my wife had bought me. The run started well; the temperature was a bit below freezing, but the warm clothes and the heat that our bodies generated when exercising made it comfortable. The road was empty. There were no runners, cyclists, or cars. Who would want to be out so early on a Sunday morning in such severe weather?

Running in ski gear

The first six miles were good, and we completed our run in less than an hour. About half an hour later, we hit the turnaround point. We were both feeling strong and going at a decent pace for those conditions, but the first strides going back explained it all. We had been running with the wind at our backs. On the return, the rolling hills up from Delaware to Pennsylvania would have a lot of headwinds that were getting stronger by the minute.

The wind chill brought the temperature to about 5° F (–15° C). I did not expect that, but quitting was not an option. The ski gear was holding up to the cold, but the gloves were the weak link. They were way too light for that weather. My hands were killing me. I'd run for a while, feel them get cold, then very cold, then I'd stop feeling them.

One of the few things that helped was to put my hands under the fleece I was running with. I would run with my arms restricted for a while until I could feel my hands again, so I could go back to running normally. It was painful and worrisome, but I kept pushing. Dani was dealing much better with the cold than I was, but he started to feel pain in his right leg. It was something weird, and he would often punch the outside of his right leg with the side of his right fist. He said it helped alleviate the pain. What a sight for the unaware driver: two guys running in wintry conditions, one of them with his hands tucked under his jacket and the other one hitting his own leg with his fist. They would probably think Dani and I were making good on a promise or something.

With about thirteen miles behind us, we passed a café that looked warm. It was one of the few shops on that whole route. We looked at each other. The unspoken question was, *Should we, for once, act like normal people and seek refuge from the cold in the cozy café?* It would help prevent Dani's injury from getting worse, and I would not get frostbite on my hands. We could also be irresponsible and continue to run to achieve a completely arbitrary distance that Dani and I had agreed on without any science or common sense, just the will to do it. It took us just a few seconds to decide. We kept running!

A few miles later, we reached the small hill that leads up to Centerville, a tiny, beautiful town close to the Pennsylvania border. The hill was small, but combined with the cold, the headwind, and the fatigue of running sixteen miles, it was too much for my body. I started to feel a strong pain in my right knee. I slowed down. Dani took off. The slower pace helped but didn't eliminate the knee pain, so I stopped running. Although I could not run the planned eighteen miles, I was not willing to cut it short, so I decided to walk the remaining miles. They were brutal and probably the worst two miles of my life. Cold, windy, and painful.

The cold was so bad that I stopped at a convenience store on the way to warm myself up. I had no money or credit card with me at the time, but the guy working at the store felt sorry for me. He approached me and said, "Look, water is free. Why don't you get some hot water to warm yourself?" Holding that cup of hot water with my frozen hands felt incredibly good. I felt them thawing. I drank the water slowly, and it helped me warm myself.

After a few minutes in the convenience store, I went back on the road and walked to the car. I had to complete what I set myself up to do, the arbitrary, nonsense eighteen miles. I did it. But something was not quite right when I arrived. Dani was hiding from the cold behind my car. He was freezing! I was the one who drove in the morning and the car keys were in my pocket. Neither Dani nor I realized that when we split up in Centerville. He was waiting for me in the cold after running eighteen miles for over an hour. Many lessons were learned that day: to have more respect for the weather; that being too aggressive about goals too early can be dangerous, to build up over time to whatever distance or pace I wanted to achieve, to take some cash when running, and to stick together when things are not looking good, just to name a few. It was a great, humbling experience for both of us.

I was exhausted from the cold running experience, but everything went away when I arrived home. My wife was waiting for me. She was furious, concerned with the decision to run in that weather and with the fact that I took much longer than I had planned for. As I was getting delayed, she started to Google what could happen when running in freezing weather, and as you can imagine, she found all kinds of things that just made her more concerned. When I arrived, she made sure to use some of what she found on the internet to scare me as well.

"Do you know people can get frostbite without feeling anything? Most times, it is irreversible. I read about a runner that didn't respect the cold weather, went for a run in Central Park, and got frostbite. On his penis! They had to amputate it! Is this the risk you want to take?"

Okay, I have to say that she got my attention. I looked at her; she wanted to show me the piece of news that covered the story, but I didn't want to read it, and I said, "You are absolutely right. This is a risk I'm not willing to take." I could see the instant relief on her face, then I continued, "So, we need to go shopping for some good cold-running gear!"

She smiled, looked at me, and said, "You are not going to stop, are you?" I shook my head. Later that day, we went clothes and glove shopping.

The run in the cold showed me for the first time what my limit was. Until that point, I had been able to achieve all the goals I set for myself, but that day, things were different. Moreover, I certainly crossed a line of personal safety. The unplanned cryotherapy changed my sensitivity to cold on my hands. Ten years later, my hands still feel cold very quickly, forcing me to wear thick gloves, sometimes multiple layers of gloves or hand warmers, even in the California cold. The good thing is that no other part of my body was affected by the cold that day.

After getting a taste of the adverse weather that was ahead of me for the upcoming three months, I got worried, and some ghosts from the past started to worry me. After many years and countless false starts, I could finally get a decent running sequence under my belt. Would I have the willpower to overcome the cold, the snow, and the short winter days, to continue training? I knew my wife's worry about the cold would not help me either. I made sure to go running on the first day of cold temperatures, but the experience was not the best. I had learned and gotten proper gear, but would this be enough? I didn't think so, so I decided to go bold and registered for a full marathon in New York's Central Park in February, the peak of winter. There was no way out. To have a chance to complete the marathon, I had to face the winter head-on!

My wife didn't really like the idea. She was concerned with the cold and wanted me to wait for a marathon in the spring or over the summer. But as I really wanted to do it, she decided to support me. Once I received the confirmation email, I forwarded it to Dani, who was not sure if he would sign up for it. He was still feeling pain in his right leg from that long, cold run, but I gave it a shot. A few minutes later, he replied. No question, no comment, nothing written on the email, just his registration attached to it. New goal, same partnership!

The real winter hit Pennsylvania, and with it, the snow. Looking through the window, the grass and the trees turning white were beautiful, and under normal circumstances, it would have been an invitation to stay home, get a glass of wine, and enjoy my warm and cozy home. But that winter was different; I was excited to see the snow and to experience training in those new conditions. I was curious beyond my back yard covered in snow. How would the places that I discovered running be covered in snow? Could I even run in the snow? With three months to go before the marathon, I knew I didn't have any time to waste, so I didn't miss a single opportunity to train. I hit the road when it was snowing, raining, or freezing. Sometimes, I managed to do it in the early mornings before work, but most times, I had to run at night, just with the moonlight.

Life didn't stop suddenly because I now had a marathon on the schedule. I had to manage all the training in parallel with work and family obligations, which is not easy, but once you are on a roll, somehow, you find a way to make it possible. I remember the day I dropped my car to change tires at Costco and used the one hour that would have been wasted waiting or checking the phone to run the perimeter of Costco's parking lot. People gave me strange looks, but I didn't care. I had to change the tires, but I also needed to get my run in, and I did both! Another day I dropped my daughter, Sophia, at a kids' birthday party at a place about thirty minutes from our home. Instead of driving back home just to drive back to the party to pick her up, I left the car at the birthday place parking lot and went running in the neighborhood. Sometimes, the area was not great for running, but it got the job done.

Juggling work, my personal life, and training was not easy, but for some reason, the harder it got to manage the schedule, the easier it was for me to train because I knew I could not miss that opportunity. It is like when you arrive at an empty parking lot and can't decide in which spot you want to park. Should you look for a shady one, one closer to the entrance, or one that is away from traffic? When you arrive at a busy parking lot and see someone leaving, you just take that spot first, then think. My agenda was a busy parking lot, so whenever I could squeeze in training, I did it. I always had running and swimming clothes in the car and I was ready to train at any time.

The workouts were getting longer and the days shorter because of the winter, so Dani and I started to use the YMCA not only for swimming but also for running on the treadmill during the week. Every workout counted. Every weekend I was going further, and by late December, I reached the 18.6 miles (30k). It was an encouraging milestone. Four months earlier, I could barely run three miles. Dani continued to struggle with his right leg injury, which required him to rest to properly recover. I was able to address the cold hands with warmer gloves and hand warmers, and during the December holidays, I could get a break from the cold as we headed to Key West.

My training plan called for a twenty-mile run, and to minimize impacting the family vacation, I decided to do it early one morning. I left around 6 a.m. and slowly and steadily did a loop of the island. Clear skies and the cool ocean breeze made the run easy and enjoyable. I have to say it was much better than running in Costco's parking lot. Key West is not a big island, so I had to go for a second loop, which was also great. I completed the run, did some stretches, and calmly walked back to my room to meet Jai and the kids. When I entered the room, my wife looked at me with a look of fear on her face and yelled, "What happened to you?" Still, in my alpha state of mind, I could not understand her reaction. She then pointed to my shirt. I slowly looked down and, to my surprise, it was covered in blood!

"I didn't get shot, or at least, I don't think I did," I said. When we looked closer, there were two main sources of blood: my nipples. Training in a much higher temperature than I was used to had some side effects. The heavy, sweaty shirt rubbing on the nipples for over three hours caused the wounds, and a lot of blood had dripped from each of them. My white shirt was in a terrifying state. Later I learned that it is common to either use anti-chafing balm on them or to cover them with some sort of Band-Aid to prevent this issue.

It was interesting that I didn't feel anything while running, while my mind was in the zone to complete the twenty miles. I was really focused and engaged in my training, but I had to be careful not to break into pieces in the process. The cold run at the beginning of the winter and the bloody run over the winter break made it clear that I still had to learn what the limits of my body were.

The marathon goal was beyond any of my wildest dreams, but it was getting close. I had been able to manage the schedule between home, work, and training, and I'd found a great training buddy. I overcame the fears and issues of running in the winter. I was determined, and surprisingly, that became my biggest challenge. Would my body cope with everything that was happening?

Running with bloody nipples was not great, but going back home without even noticing was more concerning. Was I listening to my body? I was so focused on running that it was probably blurring my vision. Around the same time, Dani called; he was unsure he would be able to run the marathon anymore. He had visited a doctor because of the pain in the right leg, the one that started on that first twenty-mile cold run. He was diagnosed with a stress fracture and had to take a break from running. He could still swim and do the elliptical at the gym, which gave him a chance to continue his preparation. I started feeling pain in my right knee after the runs. I pushed through a few times, but all the voices of the people who said that running was bad for the knees started to come up, and I decided to pay a visit to the doctor.

The doctor was also an athlete who had several marathons and tri-athlons under her belt, and after several exams, she didn't find any issue with my knee. She said I was fine to continue running. She mentioned that the discomfort was probably on the right iliotibial band, commonly known as the IT band, a part of my body that I didn't even know existed before. Still, I eventually developed an intimate relationship with it. The IT band is a ligament that connects the pelvic bone to the shinbone and is located on the outside of the leg. Many runners suffer a common running injury when the kneecap rubs on the IT band, which gets inflamed. That was the easy part of the diagnostics. The hard part was identifying the root cause of why the kneecap was sliding to the side and rubbing on the IT band, and if you talk to ten people, you may very well get ten different answers.

After describing my training routine, her number-one recommendation was to stop running on the treadmill. The unnatural stride caused several issues, and she had treated many treadmill injuries throughout her career. If I really needed to exercise indoors, she recommended using the elliptical machine instead. It was not great, but at least it gave me an alternative. She also suggested I should apply heat on my knee before running, so it would loosen the ligaments, and apply ice afterward, to help reduce inflammation.

In this process, I learned that humans were born to run. Our body is a perfect running machine; if you ever find yourself hurting during or after running, stop. This is the machine's signal that something is not right. It is better to fix the issue before it breaks down the machine. Many people may treat the symptoms, in many cases with painkillers, but this is dangerous. Painkillers may mask the issue in the short term and cause more harm in the long term. It is important to fix the issue's root cause, which sometimes can be hard to identify. To do so may require visiting different doctors and physiotherapists, but from my experience, a lot of the issues are caused by bad running form (gauge). Start with a good running coach who can assess your stride, form, stretches, and strength.

Things worked somewhat, and I continued to train over the winter, and in mid-January, I was able to train in Central Park itself. I did my longest run ever, 22.4 miles, on the marathon course. It was beautiful, the weather helped, and the run went well, but I learned that running in Central Park was not flat at all. The rolling hills caught me by surprise.

The race day was approaching quickly, and I started to taper, which means reducing the training volume so the body can properly recover and be at its peak performance for the race day. I decided to do my last run before the marathon on an indoor track at the YMCA. It was a small track that ran above and around two basketball courts. I ran about six miles, always in a clockwise direction and at a strong pace. It was my last run, and I was trying to improve my pace for the marathon. The run was fine, and I felt great, but the day after was not good, I felt that IT band pain stronger than ever. Great, a week to go before my first marathon, and my knee decided to give me a challenging time. Treadmills were bad for my IT band, but running in small circles for about an hour was not any better. The week leading up to the race included a lot of ice and hope.

The marathon preparation felt good. The long runs were done without serious issues. I managed the wintry weather, work, and family commitments, but that knee pain on the last run was not necessary. I decided to keep it to myself. My wife was the only person I had briefly talked about it with. I didn't want to give too much space in my head for the injury. My focus had to be on the marathon, on the possibility of accomplishing something that I considered unimaginable just six months before.

During the week, the pain would ease, but it never went away. The IT band was not the only concern I had to overcome. The weather was the other one. New York City had been hit with a cold front and snowstorms in the two weeks leading up to the race. Temperatures were way below freezing, and a snowstorm that weekend would most likely cancel the event.

I had bought the proper gear and learned how to train in the cold; at that point, I was ready for a winter marathon.

Aug 27 – First run   *Dec 31 – Key West run*

Chapter 9

The Central Park Marathon

"Whether you think you can or you think you can't, you're right."

—*Henry Ford, American entrepreneur*

2014

The race weekend arrived. On Saturday morning, we drove to NYC, and some great news started to appear. The weather in New York had cleared up, and Sunday was expected to be sunny and the warmest day of the winter. The athlete check-in and the trip took my mind off the IT band concern for a while. A week of icing also helped. The pain had reduced substantially. The excitement started to rise; the marathon was feeling real. Arriving at the hotel, I started to review my racing gear and my nutrition plan when my wife arrived. That was when I revealed to her that I was excited about the marathon but was not planning on stopping there. She didn't seem surprised at all until I shared what lay ahead of us.

"Look, I always loved biking and was considering adding cycling to the training schedule."

Now she knew something different was coming up, not another

marathon later that year. She looked at me and asked, "So, what are you really thinking of doing?"

Looking into her eyes, and probably with a seven-year-old's smile on my face, I asked, "Have you heard of the Ironman?"

She was in shock and could not even shake her head. She then asked me, "I know it is a triathlon, but what exactly is an Ironman? What are the distances?"

I then explained, "It starts with a 2.4-mile ocean swim, followed by a 112-mile bike ride, to finish with a 26.2-mile run, in other words, a marathon."

She started laughing, a mix of disbelief and nervousness. "You must be kidding. You have not yet done a marathon, and you don't even have a road bike." We talked for a while, but she was not agreeable at all.

Dani had recovered from his injury, and his training had been compromised, but he was still willing to venture into the marathon. Later that day, we went out with Dani and his family and, following a common running tradition, we went for a pasta dinner to load our bodies with carbohydrates before the race, what people call carb loading. I was hesitant to eat pasta, or any carb, for that matter. After many years of fighting with my weight, I had reached the once-unthinkable 174 pounds. I was not willing to risk that, not even for a better performance at the race. I ate only a small whole-grain pasta dish, not a lot of carb loading for me. The Ironman topic came back at the dinner table. My wife was treating it more as a joke. She could not believe someone in their right mind would want to do that—least of all me! Dani showed a lot of interest in the Ironman, but his wife, Rita, not so much.

Arriving back at the hotel, after putting the kids to bed, we talked one last time about the Ironman that day, and after some discussions, we agreed that if I could complete the marathon in less than four hours, I could register for the Ironman. The twenty-two miles that I did at Central Park took me three hours and fifty-one minutes. If I could keep the pace I was running at twenty-two miles, my expected marathon time was four hours and forty minutes. I knew that below four hours was an almost impossible task, but I accepted the challenge. I was confident that my extra motivation would help me overcome the issues with the IT band or any other issue that could appear. The marathon now was not the endgame. It had just become part of something bigger; it was a major steppingstone to achieve the Ironman.

With short winter days, the marathon was planned to start at 8:30 a.m., so we had time to sleep well, not that it really happened. I woke up at around 4 a.m.; the anxiety and expectation for the race didn't let me sleep any more. Then, I filled the bathtub with warm water and stayed there for a while. I really wanted to loosen up the IT band. I could still feel some discomfort on the outside of my right knee, but I had a marathon to run and an Ironman to prepare for, assuming things would go as I wanted them to go. Close to 6 a.m., Jai, Sophia, and Gabe woke up. I can't say that waking up that early was their favorite part of the race, especially on a weekend. After overcoming some (maybe a lot) of morning grumpiness, we hopped in a taxi and got to the starting line, and what a starting line it was!

Central Park was at its best. The day was bright and clear. There was not a single cloud in the sky. It was unusually warm, around 50° F (10° C), there was no wind, and the park was all covered in fresh snow from the storms earlier that week. It was so beautiful. It felt as if the park had been prepared for us with a lot of fresh snow, but the temperature rose to make the marathon more pleasant.

Dani and his family were already there, and this time, it was easy to find each other, as this was a small race, not a surprise for a marathon in New York City in February. About one hundred runners were lining up. It was a different feeling from Philly—no crowd, no confusion, no long lines for portable toilets. It was almost like an organized workout session. Dani and I went to the back of the group. Dani was quiet, preserving himself for the race. He didn't even want to walk to the portable potties to save his legs. He was unsure if he had fully recovered from the injury. I was the opposite. I wanted to stay warm, to make sure my muscles were ready to run and that I would not have any IT band issues. While he was standing still, waiting, I was doing small warmup drills to be ready for my first marathon.

After several long minutes of waiting, the race started at 8:30 a.m. sharp. I had a chance to wave to my family, blow one last kiss, and then it was time to take off. With an aggressive time target, I knew that I had not a second to spare. I started strong, stronger than I had ever run in my whole life. Dani wanted to start slow and see how his body reacted and if his leg would not fail him, but he also wanted to run side by side with me. We would run together for a little bit, then he would fall behind. I would look back at him, wave for him to join me, and then he would push the pace and catch up with me. During the first thirty minutes, I heard a dozen times, "Hey, maybe we are going too strong for a marathon." I knew I was, and that was my best chance to hit the four-hour mark, or at least, that is what I believed.

After a while, Dani gave in and said, "Okay, let's do this." It was the moment that he got his confidence back from the injury and decided to go all-in for the race as well. We did 6.2 miles in fifty-one minutes. My normal time was over an hour. We ran side by side the whole time, with some conversation, but not much, as the pace was strong for both of us. We could wave and say hi to our families a few times, as the course included five loops of Central Park. I have to say that seeing them during the first half was easy, but during the second half of the marathon, it was much harder to find them. We crossed the half marathon mark at one hour and forty-nine minutes, eight minutes faster than the half marathon in Philly. The pace was going well, and I needed to keep that till the end to be able to close it in less than four hours, but fatigue was starting to kick in.

After the first half, Dani opened up from me, and it was his time to wave for me to join him. I did it for another thirty minutes or so, but then it became unsustainable for me. Within three hours, we reached twenty miles. Six miles to go, and it had to be done in less than an hour. Things didn't look good for me.

I lost visual contact with Dani, and I started to feel extremely hungry. My stomach started to growl. I was carrying some running gels and could also get Gatorade from the aid stations, but they didn't get the job done. I wanted real food! The pretzels and hot dogs from Central Park stands never smelled so good. I swear I almost stopped at one of them to get some food, but first, I don't think the race rules would allow for that, and second, I didn't have any money either. I kept pushing harder and harder but going slower and slower.

I started focusing on the course, to make sure I didn't miss a turn, but my concentration started to fade. I remember passing a group who started to cheer, "Go, Brazil!" in Portuguese, which I thought was weird. I was trying to see if I knew them, but I didn't recognize anyone. Some miles later, I realized that I was running with the Brazilian national soccer team jersey, and that's why the fellow Brazilians were cheering me.

The small hills in Central Park were getting bigger and steeper. I lost my sense of direction. At the beginning of the race, I knew exactly where I was. The Met, the Guggenheim Museum, the Reservoir, Strawberry Fields, the zoo—everything was a clear reference for me. I knew where I was in the park and what to expect next, but after running for over three hours in circles, I lost track of where I was. I didn't know if I was on the east or west side, going north or south. I could only rely on the race signs and on following other runners. I had lost sight of Dani, and at that point, the four-hour mark was much less important. A lot of people would pass by and say encouraging words that helped me to keep going.

I didn't want to walk. I had to complete the marathon running, all 26.2 miles. With brief stops at the aid stations to get water, I continued to drag myself through the last lap of the course. Looking back at my pace on the last few miles of the marathon, I may have gone faster if I had simply walked, but at that time, I thought I was running, and after four hours and eighteen minutes, I crossed the finish line. At that point, I could barely stand. For a moment, I felt I'd just fall to the ground, but seeing Jai and the kids kept me standing.

I was so happy to cross the finish line and finally hug my family. After so much effort, the four-hour goal was just a detail on the whole thing. When my boss, Steen, learned that I was going to do a marathon, he told me something that he had learned a few years before in Switzerland. "In a marathon, when you reach twenty-three miles (thirty-seven kilometers), you will make it, but you are only halfway there!" It may not make much sense, as the marathon has twenty-six miles (forty-two kilometers), but after running one myself, I could confirm that the saying is correct. Dani went through a similar process toward the end and finished ten minutes ahead of me, but not in better condition than I was. We were both destroyed. When he saw me, the first thing he said was, "Man, are you sure about this Ironman thing? Can you imagine running what we ran today after biking 112 miles [180 kilometers]? Impossible!"

I have to say that at that moment, it was extremely hard to think of the possibility of an Ironman. I just wanted to eat something and rest. My wife had bought some bagels for the kids, and I didn't think twice; I had a couple of them right there, sitting on the ground close to the finish line. I made sure to take a picture holding both kids, Sophia and Gabe. I'm not sure where I got the strength to do that. At that point, my body was a wreck.

Despite that, I couldn't have been happier at my accomplishment, and although even the next few steps seemed impossible, I felt unstoppable in that moment!

Running with Dani

Sol and Gabe waiting for Dad

With the strength to hold
Sol and Gabe after 26.2 miles

Family picture with the
first marathon medal

CHAPTER 10

LIFE IS A BEAUTIFUL RIDE

"Nature is pleased with simplicity."
—*Sir Isaac Newton, English physicist*

2014

The sub-four-hours marathon didn't come, but I still wanted to do the Ironman; it felt like the natural next step on the journey, but I was not alone on that journey. A few weeks after the marathon, I drove my wife and kids to JFK airport in New York, and we talked about the Ironman on the way, but the three-hour drive was not long enough. We arrived at the airport before an agreement, and the rush to check the luggage and get to the gate took priority. When it was time to say goodbye, Jai, maybe motivated by the long discussion in the car and probably feeling a bit guilty for going on vacation with the kids to Brazil while I was at work, turned to me, looked into my eyes, and said, "Okay, I know you really want to do an Ironman, and Cozumel seems a fun place to go, so, if you get a coach, I'm in!"

These were her last words before boarding a twelve-hour flight to Brazil, which gave me plenty of time to drive back home and register for Ironman Cozumel 2014, before she or I changed our minds. The next morning, she landed in Brazil, called me, and her first question was, "So, are we going to Cozumel in November?" After my *"Yes!"* she asked her second question, "Did you already get a coach?"

I answered, "Not yet; first I need to get a bike!"

She started laughing and said, "You are probably the only person that registered for an Ironman who doesn't already have a bike."

It was March, and it was still too cold to ride outside in Pennsylvania, but I started shopping around for a bike, to be more precise, for a tri-bike, that's what people call the time trial bicycles used for triathlons.

In most triathlon races, drafting is not allowed, meaning that you can't ride behind another athlete or a group of athletes to avoid air resistance. The other main difference is that most triathlon courses are flat or rolling hills. There are no challenging climbs like the ones on cycling races. To optimize for those conditions, the tri-bike design prioritizes aerodynamics over weight. The tri-bike also includes aero bars, which are two bars attached to the handlebar and sticking out to the front of the bike, allowing the athlete to stay at a lower position, further reducing the wind resistance.

The gear shifters are positioned on the aero bars, as that is the position in which a triathlete stays most of the time, but while on the aero bars, control of the bike is limited. The athlete should not get off the saddle, make turns, or brake, especially because the brake levers are on the normal handlebars, not on the aero bars. In a traditional tri-bike, you either have access to gear shifters or to the brake levers, not both at the same time; that's why you don't see tri-bikes riding as part of a Peloton or group rides.

In summary, the tri-bike is heavier and way more difficult to handle than a normal road bike, and the aero position can be dangerous and uncomfortable, especially for the lower back. For all these reasons, I heard from nearly everyone that I talked to that I should start with a traditional road bike, use it for a season or two, then move to a tri-bike. So, what did I do? Of course, I got a tri-bike!

First of all, I didn't have a season or two before the Ironman, and my mind was set. I had one goal: finish Ironman Cozumel. I was not looking to become a cyclist, do group rides, or climb hills. Ironman Cozumel was a flat course, and a tri-bike was surely the best choice for that type of race and course. If I wanted to do the race, that was the bike! For me, it seemed logical to use the same bike for the training from the beginning. I could not get my head around adjusting to one bike and then adjusting to a second bike later on.

In April, when the weather improved, I got my bike and did the proper bike fitting to make sure the saddle and handlebar positions were correct for me, which is much harder on a tri-bike than it sounds because of the aero bars and the aero position. I did some test rides near my home during the week and prepared for my first real ride over the weekend. Talking to some folks, I learned that the best place to train for a flat course would be to take Delaware Route 9, which was the old road to the shore that was nearly empty since everyone now took the new and faster road to the shore. Without any science, I set myself the target of riding fifty miles, not knowing exactly what to expect.

On Saturday, I woke up at 5 a.m., got my bike and gear in the car, and drove to Delaware City, which was the starting point for my first real ride. I set a twenty-five-mile out-and-back course along Route 9 and started. The bike was great, and the aero position was not so bad. The fact that the road was empty removed any safety concerns. I rode nonstop to the twenty-five-mile mark, turned around, and rode back, learning the various positions, gears, etc. After almost three hours of riding, I was reaching my fifty-mile goal, and it felt good, in fact, too good to stop then. Arriving back at the car, I decided to extend the ride and rode for an additional twelve miles, completing sixty-two miles (100k) on my first ride. It felt fantastic.

Like swimming, biking was special for several reasons. First, I had the same feeling that I could just keep going effortlessly, forever. I wish one day I could say this about running. Second, it also brought back a lot of childhood memories. Before my dad lost his job and we stopped traveling to the country house, I used to spend most of my weekend on a bike. I'd always be the first to wake up, ride to my friends' house, knock on their windows to wake them up, and then we would leave on day-long rides. Sometimes, we would take the dirt roads that would often lead us to different small towns and waterfalls. It was great, beautiful, and peaceful, but there was a route that I liked even more.

There were some landslides on the state road that passed close to the house. The first of them was just a couple of hundred meters away from my house. There were two more after that, about six and twelve miles from our house. The state maintained the road, or it would be better to say it was not maintained at all. The landslides stayed there, blocking the road for all my childhood years.

It was difficult for the people who needed to use the road; they had to use poorly created detours that often got blocked as well, and people ended up just avoiding the road altogether. It was a hassle for the communities that depended on that road, as it created a major challenge for an economy that needed tourism to prosper, but it was heaven for us kids to ride our bikes. No traffic, no danger. We would just enjoy the smooth ride on the pavement, the high speed on the downhills, and the wind in our faces; we had not even heard about cycling helmets. We would ride all day long and stop at different snack bars, shops, and places with nice views.

Riding allowed me to cover much more ground than running, and it was a completely distinct experience than being in a car. On the bike, you experience the weather conditions, breathe the fresh air, and enjoy the scents and sounds of nature. At a much lower speed, I could note so many more details around me: the hills, the creeks, the trees, and the wildlife. Biking got me even more connected with nature, with all life around me, and ultimately, with myself.

Despite being comfortable and confident on the bike, it was the last sport I was picking up with only a few months to go for the Ironman, and it represented the longest part of the race, 112 miles, so I decided to look for a coach who had a stronger background in cycling, and of course, I got the referral at the local bike shop.

The coach helped plan the season leading up to the Ironman and helped structure my weekly training plan, something much more complex with three sports in the mix. To help manage the schedule constraints, she recommended getting an indoor bike trainer. Basically, a device that lifts the bike's rear wheel from the floor and gives some resistance to it, allowing you to ride your own bike as a stationary bike. Remember all those great feelings that I mentioned about cycling? None of them apply when you are riding in a confined space, say your basement, staring at the wall. But the indoor trainer was unavoidable. It was efficient, and the flexibility to use it at any time of the day or night made it worth it.

Riding brought me closer to nature, gave me the opportunity to learn more about the community I was living in, and brought back the great memories from my childhood. Life was great then and was starting to become great again!

New bike

Warming up on the bike trainer for a race

CHAPTER 11

THE HEALER

"Awareness is the first step in healing."
—*Dean Ornish, American physician*

2014

Things were happening fast. In eight months, I had dropped over eighty pounds, run the Philly half marathon, Central Park Marathon, completed a half Ironman distance triathlon in Connecticut, and was swimming, running, and cycling over six hundred miles per month. The accelerated pace was great for my motivation, but not so great for my body. In the last long run before my second marathon, I pulled a muscle in my right calf. I let it rest to recover, but with only two weeks left before the race, I didn't have much time. In hindsight, I should have pulled out of the race, but instead, I decided to do it at an easy pace, but still do it. It worked for eighteen miles, but when I faced the second hill of the course, my calf went on a spasm—like a strong cramp, but on the whole muscle group, and I could not relax it. It was so painful. I managed to drag myself limping to the finish line.

It took me six weeks to fully recover from the injury, but just when I thought things were set, an old issue reappeared, and this time, much stronger: the IT band syndrome. The inflammation in my right knee was getting worse by the day, to the point that I was not able to run even three miles. I visited different doctors. Some blamed it on overuse, others on muscle imbalance due to the amount of cycling I had to do during the calf injury recovery period. Truth be told, no one really knew the root cause or the solution. Some suggested physiotherapy, which I was doing, but it was not working; others suggested metal braces for the knees, and others suggested surgery to adjust the position of the IT band, so it would not rub on the kneecap anymore.

With two months of training left before the Ironman, things were looking quite bad, and I started testing different shoes, insoles, bands, tapes, anything you can find in a running shop. Nothing would work for me, but on one of these visits, probably the fifth one in the same week, the shop owner stopped by to talk to me. Once he learned I had an IT band issue, he immediately said, "You should see my brother. He works with athletes and has resolved many IT band issues before." His brother was known in the region as "the Healer." That's exactly what I needed.

I exchanged some emails with the Healer, but I hesitated. I was unsure if seeing another specialist was a promising idea. I was getting fatigued with so many different opinions, and getting one more opinion could do more harm than good. After reflecting, I wrote to let him know that I had decided to continue with the current treatment and would not see him at that time. He then replied, "IT band issues can be resolved in forty-eight hours once you get the science right. And do not use foam rollers; they will make it worse."

My IT Band had been an issue for much longer than forty-eight hours, and the home exercises prescribed by the physiotherapist did include the foam roller. His answer was too intriguing to let go, so I decided to take one last opinion and scheduled an appointment for that same week.

The Healer's office was a small room in an office building in downtown Philadelphia with no luxury or fancy equipment, just a physiotherapy table, some straps, some rubber bands, and a big mirror leaning on the wall. That was all he used. It was simple, raw. We started with a lot of discussion and analysis.

He wanted to know my story, my training grounds, my habits, and my goals. It was clearly different from the other doctors I had been to. He was trying to understand who I was and what the main root causes were for my issues. He was not following the standard procedures for someone with IT band issues. He tested my flexibility and range of motion. One thing was clear: My IT band was extremely inflamed. The runs, physiotherapy, painful Graston sessions, and foam roller were all adding to the inflammation. He did a lot of massage to loosen the IT band and taught me some different stretches using a strap to help improve my flexibility, as it was really bad.

The session, which was planned for one hour, went way over, and we spent nearly two hours talking, doing the massage, and the strength and stretch exercises. In the end, he prescribed an extensive workout routine for me, with stretches and strengthening exercises twice a day, and I needed to do them for at least six weeks. Luckily, I was eight weeks away from the race and still had time to recover so I could do it well.

Close to the end of the session, he turned to me and said, "Pain is a signal to the brain that something is not right. Sometimes, this signal can be wrong, and one can feel pain where there is no pain. This might happen when the pain a person feels was really strong or if a person is suffering pain for a long time." That was interesting, but he didn't stop there and continued, "The opposite can also be true. There are cases where the person should have pain, but the brain just doesn't understand the signal or learns to ignore it, which can be dangerous and can cause severe injuries." Okay, now he was starting to scare me, but the best part was yet to come. "And there are things that you can do to trick your brain, so it learns to ignore certain pain, even though the pain is still there, but one has to be careful when to use it."

He told me some cases that he worked with where the cause of the pain was cured, but the person continued to feel it until they tricked their brain. He offered to teach me one trick that could be helpful for me, but only if I was certain the cause of the pain had been resolved, otherwise it could do me more harm than good.

I took his offer. He asked me to grab the mirror that was leaning on the wall and sat on the chair. Then he asked me to hold the mirror with my hand in between my knees in a position where the mirror would reflect my left knee, which was the knee without any pain. At the same time, the mirror should block my vision to my right knee, the one with the IT band issue. The idea was to find the ideal position where I could see my left knee and its reflection in the mirror in front of me without seeing my right knee. I had to trick my brain into thinking that the reflection was my right knee.

After finding an acceptable position with the mirror, he asked me to stare at the reflection for a while, then gently touch my left knee with my left hand. I should not look or focus on what was happening on the left side; instead, I should keep staring at the reflection of the left knee in the mirror. I should not think too much about it; I needed to make it natural. The last thing I should try to do was try to convince myself that the left knee image in the mirror was my right knee. I should only look at the image and accept it as is, feel it, and let the mind wander, staring at that image. As my focus on the left knee reduced, I started to massage it, then rubbed my hand on the outside part of the knee, on the IT band. That time, I was feeling no pain. Of course, I was rubbing the left knee, but the image showed me as if it was the right one.

It was strange in the beginning, but after ten to fifteen minutes, everything felt more natural. There was no left or right. There was no mirror. I kept touching, massaging, and rubbing for a while, letting my mind wander, and letting my brain associate that with my right knee. I needed to create paths in my brain that associated my right knee with comfort, breaking the ones that were created before associating it with pain. Toward the end, I just closed my eyes, returned the mirror to him, stretched, and started to move.

It was a strange feeling. It was different. I could not feel my right knee or any pain at all. The whole exercise took about thirty minutes and changed my perception of pain, but I knew the pain was still there. The Healer told me that the pain would come back and that training the brain may take some time, so for this technique to really work, I would have to do a similar session several times, preferably in different settings, making sure the brain associates the right knee with an injury-free knee.

Again, doing that without fixing the knee for real was dangerous and not recommended, as it could cause severe injuries. I was glad to have learned the technique and, at the same time, intrigued by how much power one's brain really has, but I decided not to use it. Instead, I focused on strengthening and stretching routines to get in good shape for the race. The visit to the Healer gave me a lot of hope, but it also gave me a lot to do! My busy days just got two more sessions of exercises, for which the Healer was emphatic: "Smile while you do it and associate them with positive thoughts and feelings."

My days started now at 5 a.m. with recovery exercises, normally done in the basement of my home, the same place the days would end, around 10 p.m., with the same recovery exercises. Despite the busy schedule, sleep quality was still good. I always felt well recovered in the morning.

More than improving flexibility and strength, the session and the exercises from the Healer increased my awareness of my body, mind, and how both are strongly connected. I always saw running as something hard, a challenge to overcome, different from how I saw swimming and cycling. Could I change my perspective on running and one day feel that I could run nonstop? Time will tell, but things changed after that session. The week after I was able to run 6.2 miles without pain, and the distance just went up from there. The Ironman was approaching quickly, and I started to believe I had a chance to be ready for it.

CHAPTER 12

HOME STRETCH

"The will to prepare has to be greater than the will to win."
—*Bernardinho, Brazilian volleyball coach*

2014

Four weeks before the race was also my final weekend with the bike before shipping it to Cozumel. Despite unfavorable late October weather—cold temperatures and fierce winds—I didn't want to miss my last opportunity for a long ride. Crosswinds threatened to push me off the road, but I didn't give up. The impact of the wind on cycling was more intense than I anticipated, exacerbating the cold, and attempting to ride faster to generate warmth only made it worse—an unpleasant experience. Though I completed the ride, the consequences were immediate: I developed a cold that week, just as I had planned to do my last long run.

The eighteen-mile run was crucial for my final preparation and confidence boost before the race. I planned to run it in Philly immediately after shipping my bike to Cozumel, choosing a mix of city paths and trails to minimize strain on the knees. The goal was to finish at the Rocky Balboa statue, mirroring the successful finish of my half marathon in Philadelphia. It was a solid plan, but my body was still recovering from the cold I caught riding in freezing wind the previous weekend.

Faced with few options, I had to choose between allowing my body more recovery time or sticking to the training plan. I opted for the latter. Giving up was never an option for me. At that time, I believed that cutting a workout short or skipping one due to feeling unwell would mark the beginning of failure. Now, I place a higher value on recovery than I did back then.

Saturday arrived—a beautiful day with sunshine, no wind, and relatively warm for that time of year. It was a stark contrast to the previous weekend. I woke up early, drove into the city, dropped off my bike, grabbed some food to fuel my eighteen-mile run, and parked near the art museum. It was time to validate all my preparation, confirm that the Healer's stretches had worked, that my IT band wasn't an issue anymore, and that I was truly ready for the Ironman. Reality, however, fell far short of my expectations.

The run was grueling from the start. I felt fatigued early on, and it only worsened with each mile. Despite this, I was determined not to let a cold derail my efforts to finish my training on a high note—until it did. Around seven miles, things became exceptionally tough. I remember calling my wife, hoping she and the kids would meet me near the Rocky Steps in about an hour. It was a bid for extra motivation to persevere through the difficulty and still achieve what I had set out to do. She was occupied with the children, and my invitation wasn't compelling enough.

Despite this setback, I refused to give up. I pushed on for another couple of miles, but with ten miles, I started feeling terrible and was overcome with strong nausea. I tried to continue, but the nausea intensified to the point where I nearly vomited. I had no choice but to stop. Things were getting better, but there was still a lot of work for me to do to learn to listen to my body.

I found a rock to sit on, trying to control the nausea and regain my composure. While my body gradually improved, it was a tough moment for me. I had dedicated so much time and effort, completely changing my lifestyle, and overcoming injuries over the past three months. Yet, due to a simple cold, I had just lost my final chance to complete a long run before my first Ironman. It was overwhelming, and I couldn't hold back the emotions—I sat on that giant rock in the middle of nowhere and let the tears drain my emotions out. It was a mixture of fear about facing the race underprepared and anger at wanting to train more but knowing my body had reached its limit for the day.

I spent nearly thirty minutes there, and not a single hiker passed by on what should have been a busy trail. Eventually, I decided to finish the distance walking. It took me about two hours, but it was worth it. The solitude of the long walk gave me time to reflect and recover both physically and emotionally. When I reached the Rocky Steps, I didn't sprint up them as I had originally planned. Instead, I walked slowly, counting each of the seventy-two famous steps, one by one. At the top, I savored the stunning views of the city, soaking in the vibrant energy of Philadelphia.

Later, I drove back home. It was a personal moment of reflection and solitude.

The last long run and ride hadn't gone as planned, but I still felt strong in the water. During training, I completed a few lengthy swim sessions, achieving the Ironman swim distance of 2.4 miles in about one hour and twenty minutes—a personal best. However, as the race approached, I pushed harder on the pace, which resulted in shoulder pain. I had to scale back and focus on chiropractic sessions instead of intensifying my training. I managed to get over training injuries in all three sports, but it was not over yet.

Before heading to Cancun, I stopped by Dani's house to check how he was doing. He had just completed another marathon, and his injury had come back stronger. He was using crutches. That image was impactful; hard to say that it did not impact my confidence going into my first Ironman.

The flight to Cancun was smooth. From there, we traveled by transport to Playa Del Carmen and then took the ferry to Cozumel. My wife remembers the ferry less fondly, as she felt seasick—a result of choppy waters. Despite initial concerns about swimming conditions potentially affecting the race length, the forecast suggested improving weather throughout the week. My main worry was whether adverse conditions could lead to a shortened or canceled swim. I had trained for a full Ironman; I wanted that, not a shortened version. No shortcuts.

Arriving in Cozumel was memorable. Upon disembarking the ferry, a large sign greeted us: "Welcome Ironman Athletes!" This was the first of many signs. On our way to the hotel, the island's main square had transformed into Ironman Village, adorned with large banners and infrastructure supporting the race. Hotels and restaurants proudly welcomed athletes. The entire island seemed to revolve around the Ironman event that week, creating a welcoming atmosphere that made me feel like a true athlete.

Sophia and Gabe at Cozumel's main square (Parque Municipal de Cozumel)

We headed straight to the hotel to rest from the trip and to meet my dad, who had flown all the way from Brazil to Cozumel to support me in the race. In his own words, "I can't imagine someone doing an Ironman, even less my son, so I had to come and see this happening with my own eyes." My dad, who had struggled with weight his whole life and had never practiced any sport, let alone run a 5K, viewed everything I was doing as completely insane. Despite his initial objections when I signed up for the race, even suggesting I might have serious mental problems (maybe he was right), he was there to encourage me and support our family. His presence made me feel more confident, knowing that Jai and the kids would not be alone in a foreign country while I raced.

After a good night's sleep, it was time to get organized. The days leading up to the race were hectic. First, I had to retrieve my bike, which had arrived safely, and reassemble some parts that I had removed for transport. Then, it was time for athlete check-in, where I received my bib number, an athlete bracelet I had to wear all week, race perks, and countless transition bags.

Ironman is a demanding race, and to swim 2.4 miles, bike 112 miles, and run 26.2 miles back-to-back, with no rest or external support, logistics are crucial. Each bag had a specific purpose: the pre-race bag for morning clothes before the swim, the "swim to bike" transition bag for all biking gear, shoes, helmet, goggles, sunscreen, and nutrition, a biking extra support bag available at a specific point on the course, the "bike to run" transition bag for running gear, and a running extra support bag similarly available along the course.

I had a general idea for packing the transition bags but was unsure about the others. Even for the transition bags, I struggled with decisions on nutrition, sunscreen, salt pills, bike tools, spare tires, and tubes. Packing these bags for my first race was far from a relaxing experience. The next day, after several attempts at packing and repacking, I gave up and headed to the swim course for a practice session. The ocean conditions had significantly improved over the past two days, alleviating my concern about a cancellation or shortened swim. Now, my main worry was my shoulder pain.

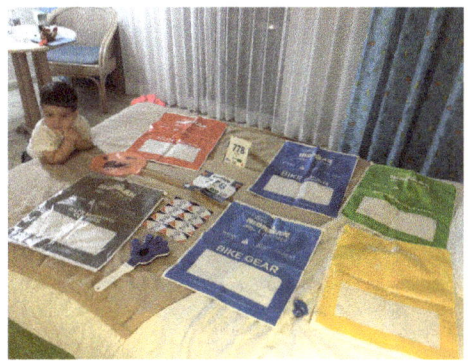 

Lots of bags   *Luckily, I had good help*

Since the pain started, I had taken a break from swimming and undergone chiropractic sessions. I warmed up thoroughly before entering the water, did shoulder exercises to loosen up, and started swimming slowly, gradually increasing my pace. I focused on enjoying the water and the moment, not worrying about my speed. Thankfully, the rest and chiropractic sessions had paid off, and I didn't feel any discomfort in my shoulder.

One of the main reasons I chose Ironman Cozumel was for the swimming. I had visited the island with my parents twenty-five years earlier for snorkeling and fell in love with the water there. This time was no different—the water was stunningly blue, with excellent visibility, comfortably warm, calm, and teeming with marine life. Could it get any better? Yes, it could! There was also a favorable current along the course, making it perfect.

Next on the agenda was familiarizing myself with the bike course. The plan was to complete one lap of the three-lap course. Our group gathered near the swim-to-bike transition and received directions from the race organizers. Within minutes, we were cycling along the south part of the island. It was breathtaking—clear skies, azure waters, white sand beaches, and a gentle ocean breeze on a nearly deserted road. I felt confident on the bike, having had no issues during training, but around twenty-four miles I felt a twinge in my right quad, near my knee. I had just shifted to a higher gear to increase speed, but it didn't agree with my quad. I quickly shifted back to an easier gear; the pain subsided, but I stopped to check my knee. I couldn't believe what had happened. After examining my knee for a few minutes, I decided to ride back to the hotel at a slow pace. I tested higher gears a few times, but each time, I felt discomfort in my knee. It was unfamiliar. It was concerning.

Entering the race, I knew my run was compromised by IT band issues, but I was counting on a strong swimming and biking performance. My plan was to complete those legs with good times, leaving room to manage the run—perhaps walking if necessary. However, that pinch in my knee had thrown everything off. Returning to the hotel, I felt devastated. I applied ice to my knee and wondered if I should or could even attempt the race just forty-eight hours away. For the rest of the day, I focused on rest and recovery, hoping a good night's sleep would alleviate the discomfort. It didn't, and on the morning before the race, my knee still bothered me, and the image of Dani wearing crutches after pushing too hard on another marathon would often come back to my mind.

I had kept my concerns to myself until that morning, but they were mounting. During breakfast with Jai and my dad, I finally voiced them. Their reactions were opposites. My dad, always worried about the race, immediately said, "You don't have to do this. It's crazy. You could risk permanent injury." Jai looked at me and said, "You're probably just nervous and unintentionally making excuses." Great. Less than twenty-four hours before starting an Ironman race and with knee pain, my wife thought I was afraid of the challenge, while my dad thought I was stupid for trying to do it. And the kids? Sophia and Gabe just wanted to play with their dad. I spent the morning with them on the beach, trying to relax, but it was difficult. After lunch, I decided to take a break.

I retreated to my room to be alone for a while, hoping to clear my thoughts and relax my mind. As I settled in, I noticed a large mirror on the bedroom wall, recalling the mind tricks I had learned from the Healer two months earlier. Without hesitation, I decided to try them. Carefully lifting the mirror off the wall, I positioned it beside my bed, aligning it with my legs so that it reflected my left knee in place of my right. For what felt like an eternity, I massaged and gently touched my left knee, losing track of time in the process.

The session brought me a profound sense of relaxation. After setting the mirror back on the wall, I indulged in a deep, rejuvenating nap that surpassed the night's sleep. Nearly three hours later, I woke up feeling refreshed and rejuvenated, though not entirely cured; it seemed I needed more practice with the Healer's techniques. The pain in my knee had lessened considerably, yet it lingered. However, my mind was clearer and calmer than before. Realizing it was time for a decision I should have made the day prior, I resolved to see a doctor.

After a few phone calls, I managed to secure an appointment at one of the island's urgent care centers, agreeing to pay two hundred pesos (about fifteen US dollars at the time) in cash, due to the late hour and the doctor's need to travel from home. There I was, at 7 p.m., the night before my first Ironman race, waiting patiently at urgent care for the doctor to examine my knee. Surprisingly, I felt remarkably calm. Shortly thereafter, the doctor arrived and introduced himself warmly, saying, "Hello, my name is Jesus, and I'm here to help you."

While I'm not particularly religious, despite my education in Christian schools, I found the moment intriguing. My inner engineer rationalized that perhaps half the men on the island were named Jesus, but in that moment, I silenced those rational thoughts and appreciated the doctor's dedication to helping me during this uncertain time.

Dr. Jesus conducted a thorough examination of my knee using just his hands, as no imaging was available. He asked me to bend my knee at various angles and applied pressure to different areas, all straightforward yet profound in their simplicity. After completing his examination as best he could under the circumstances, Dr. Jesus looked at me and calmly remarked, "Your knee is slightly inflamed, and I can't pinpoint the exact cause right now. However, I don't see any major risk for the race tomorrow. You may have to endure some discomfort, but I'm confident you'll be able to finish."

Those words were like music to my ears. I wasn't afraid of enduring pain; my primary concern was avoiding irreversible damage to my body. With Dr. Jesus giving me the green light to proceed, who was I to question it?

After the consultation, I reached into my wallet to get the two hundred pesos as agreed via phone with the urgent care assistant. At that moment, Jesus stopped me and said not to worry about the payment. He mentioned he hadn't done anything significant and that I didn't need to pay. I looked him in the eyes and said, "I'm doing an Ironman tomorrow. I don't know what's going to happen, but the last thing I want is to be in debt to Jesus. Please accept my payment." After a lot of laughter, my persistence worked, and he agreed to accept half of the payment. With everything settled with Dr. Jesus, it was time for me to run back to the hotel and share the news with my family.

Everyone was relieved, and the excitement about the race took over the atmosphere. With less than twelve hours before the race started, there was only one thing left to do: rest. I went to bed at 9 p.m. and set the alarm for 4 a.m., but it wasn't needed at all. At midnight, I woke up and couldn't sleep anymore; the anxiety about the race was too high. I tried to get back to sleep for several hours, but I couldn't stop thinking about the race. At 3 a.m., I called the night done and started to prepare myself. I took a warm shower to loosen my muscles, put on my triathlon race kit, filled the water bottles, had a light breakfast, and packed some food to eat right before the race. My wife woke up to help me out, but we had agreed not to wake the kids. We knew it was going to be a long day, and the more they could rest that morning, the better it would be for them to enjoy the Ironman experience. The plan was for them to arrive in time to see me complete the swim at the first transition area, or T1.

At 4:30 a.m., it was time to kiss my family and start what I expected to be the hardest day of my life. Despite the early hour, the hotel corridors were already bustling with people, and I quickly realized that I wasn't alone on this journey. At 5 a.m., I hopped on the race bus, and the time had come.

Preparing for the Ironman demanded meticulous planning, rigorous training, and unwavering dedication. I gave it everything I had, balancing my swimming, cycling, and running sessions. My support system helped keep my nutrition levels up. Regular rest and recovery kept me from burning out, and I finally felt like I was ready for the big day! To the Ironman!

CHAPTER 13

THE IRONMAN

"If you can dream it, you can do it."
—*Walt Disney, American entrepreneur*

2014

I took the first bus to the starting line; it was half full, and each person on that bus had a unique personal journey that led them there. Being on that bus with other athletes made me feel at home and connected. There were many first-timers who, like me, wanted to get there early and also, like me, had not slept at all the previous night. Everyone was awake and friendly, creating a welcoming environment.

Very few people enter an Ironman to cross the finish line first— maybe twenty-five out of the twenty-five hundred athletes have that aspiration. For the other 99 percent, winning has a different meaning. The race itself is the reward for a personal journey, and just being there, ready for the race, is a reason to celebrate. Completing the distances is another milestone, and the ultimate victory is, of course, completing the distances within the cutoff times, especially if it is one's first race. The Ironman is a personal journey to overcome one's mental and physical limits; it is a race against oneself, not against others.

After about twenty minutes on the bus, we arrived at T1 (Transition one) for the final setup of the bike. It was time to check the tire pressure one last time, place the filled water bottles, and load the food containers. T1 is always located at the end of the swim course and the beginning of the run course. In Cozumel, we had a point-to-point swim course, which makes swimming more interesting, but the logistics are a bit more complex. After doing the final setup in T1, I took another transport to the swim start, and there I could start feeling the tension building up. Swimming is the reason most people avoid triathlon, especially when it is in the ocean, due to the fear of currents, waves, wind, and of course, sharks and other sea creatures. Thankfully, I grew up by the ocean and learned to respect it, not fear it, and the conditions that morning were perfect. The wind from the beginning of the week was gone, the ocean was completely flat, and the water was blue, clear, and warm.

I was looking forward to the swim mass start, where twenty-five hundred people get in the water at the same time, but in previous years, there had been several issues and complaints with that type of start, especially in Cozumel, where everyone had to use a narrow ladder to exit the water. In some years, this had created a line of finishers trying to get to T1. So that year, the race directors implemented a wave start to avoid those incidents. The different age groups were staggered by a few minutes, avoiding people hitting each other in the water. When my age group was up, I was there, ready to go, and happy to be in that water. The horn to start the race has the incredible power to make someone leave any worry, concern, or stress behind. I didn't need to think about the logistics, the risks, the fears, the injuries—it was time for me to connect with the course, do my best, and enjoy it.

The first part of the course had some current going against us, but a mile into the course, a favorable current took over and made the swim as nice as it could be, all ornamented by beautiful coral reefs and some tropical fishes that were not afraid of the twenty-five hundred swimmers passing by. I could certainly swim there all day. At some point, I passed a man swimming breaststroke, wearing a scuba mask. Yes, you read that correctly—a scuba mask, not swimming goggles. He was having a blast. I'm sure his definition of having a great time didn't relate at all to how long it would take him to complete the race.

With a long day ahead of me, I took it easy on the swim, enjoyed every stroke, alternated breathing sides, and quickly got into that relaxed state of mind. I loved it. I was able to complete the swim in 1:10, ten minutes faster than my time when I swam the same distance in the pool. I left the water and immediately saw my family waving and shouting my name. It was amazing. The swim was also the part of the race that concerned my dad the most. He had asked me several times, "How many times have you swum 2.4 miles in your life?" No matter how many times I said the swim was not a concern, his fear that I'd get too tired and drown made the swim the scariest part of the day for him. When I stopped to high-five the kids, he immediately asked me, "How do you feel?" I could see his face change completely with my answer: "Like new!" I was off to a great start!

I took the time in T1 to take a quick freshwater shower, apply sunscreen, rehydrate, and hug my family before getting on the bike. It was time for the three laps of thirty-seven miles each on the southern part of the island. And to my surprise, each lap was quite different. With 112 miles ahead of me, I had planned to monitor my heart rate, reducing the pace if needed to ensure I didn't exceed 145 beats per minute. It was a good plan, but for some reason, my watch would not show my heart rate after the swim. I believe the amount of Body Glide I used to avoid chafing prevented the heart rate chest strap from making proper contact with my body. Bottom line, I was left without the key piece of information I had planned my race around. At that point, I could only follow my intuition.

I was feeling strong at the beginning of the bike. I had just finished the swim with a respectable time, and the knee pain that started two days before the race was manageable. I could feel it, but every time it started to bother me, I would push harder with my left leg, change my position on the saddle, or just use a lighter gear, and the small discomfort would go away. The first loop on the island went well, and I completed the thirty-eight miles in about two hours and five minutes. However, the weather conditions started to change.

With the sun growing stronger throughout the day, the temperature began to rise quickly, making the course more challenging. The rapid temperature change on land turned the cool ocean breeze into intense winds, much stronger than forecasted, and the wind came from a different direction. What was supposed to be a race with some crosswind (bad) and some tailwind (great) turned into a headwind race (worse). The second loop on the island was different, much harder and slower.

The only good thing was that the part of the course with the strongest winds was the most beautiful, with the turquoise Caribbean water gently kissing the white-sand beaches. The scenery helped me remain positive during the hardest parts of the bike course. With a much lower speed than normal, I could admire the different shades of blue in that stunning water, some caused by the rocks at the bottom of the ocean, others by the few clouds in the sky. At one point, I counted seven beautiful shades at the same time. To keep myself engaged and motivated, I decided to "write a book" in my mind while riding. I knew I still had a long time to overcome all that wind.

The first chapter of the book explained how the few clouds in the sky, the rock and sand bottoms, and the different depths of the ocean created those beautiful shades. I then moved on to "write" about the different people I encountered along the race and their stories. I went back and started to "write" about my experience training and my experiences with my family. The bike course turned into a big blank sheet of paper that different thoughts and memories started to populate. I called it *Seven Shades of Blue*, and it helped take my mind off the worries about the race, the wind, and the injuries. It made a strong headwind ride enjoyable, allowing me to appreciate the people and nature around me.

And nature was fair—the wind affected everyone. I was not the only one forced to slow down. It was like someone had pressed a button on a remote control, and the whole race seemed to move in slow motion. In an Ironman race, drafting is illegal; you have to stay at least a certain distance from the bike in front, and if you get closer, you must overtake the bike within a limited time, or you can be penalized and eventually disqualified. With the strong wind, people tried to minimize overtaking; no one wanted to waste more energy fighting the wind. But about four hours into the bike course, something unexpected happened.

I was there, battling the increasing wind, riding much slower than I had anticipated but still in my aero position to minimize drag. All the other athletes were doing the same thing—all but one. Suddenly, I saw this guy riding off his saddle as if he were climbing a steep mountain. He wasn't in slow motion like me or the others; he passed all of us in a heartbeat. He was flying. Yes, that was the race leader and eventual winner of the 2014 Cozumel Ironman, Michael Weiss. He was on his third and final lap on the bike course, overtaking all of us who were still on the second lap. It took over twenty minutes for the second and third places to overtake me, which happened close to the finish line. For them, the finish line was near, but for me, it was still thirty-eight miles away. I was just starting my third lap, and it started well.

After almost five hours of riding, I saw my family cheering for me for the first time—it felt good. Everyone celebrated, and it was a lot of fun, but it was also extremely fast. The only thing I could say was, "I'm good," and I'm not even sure they heard it. My wife always reminds me that if I think doing an Ironman is hard, I should try cheering for someone at a race, entertaining the kids all day under the sun for a few short moments of enthusiasm every couple of hours. After the second of these moments, I started my last bike lap. It was good to have a break from the wind on the protected west side of the course, but that part goes by quickly. Before I knew it, I was back to the windy and slow side of the course, and I went back to *Seven Shades of Blue* to help me endure the grueling riding conditions.

After so many miles battling the heat and the wind, my body started to complain as well. The worst parts were not my legs or my butt, as many would think. For me, the worst parts were my shoulders and neck. The aero position puts a lot of pressure on both, but with such a strong headwind, there was no good option. Staying on the aero bars was painful; staying off the aero bars was way too hard and slow. Even with *Seven Shades*, things started to get hard mentally. It was difficult to keep all negativity away, and some unwelcome thoughts would trickle in. *Do I have any chance now with all this time lost on the bike? Is it worth going through all this suffering? Why does anyone care? Why do I care? What was I thinking when I decided to do this race?* Every time these thoughts arose, I would keep my head down, push harder, and start a new chapter of *Seven Shades*. There were many chapters.

I expected to complete the bike portion in about six hours, but the wind blew the plan away, and after cycling for a total of seven hours and forty-two minutes, I saw my family for the second time on the bike course as I crossed the finish line—what a relief! They were there cheering alongside hundreds of other fans who were watching the race.

A few meters after crossing the finish line, a volunteer approached to retrieve my bike. Without realizing exactly what I was doing, I lifted my bike as if it were a trophy, looking directly at my family, celebrating with them that the 112-mile bike course was behind me. The entire crowd who had been cheering erupted in excitement. What an incredible experience.

After less than sixty seconds of celebration, it was time for me to keep moving. I still had a full marathon ahead of me. I grabbed my T2 (Transition two) bag, entered the changing room, and prepared for the next 26.2 miles of my Ironman journey. After kissing my family, I set off on the run—a very long run. I was happy to be running, relieved to be off my bike, but within five minutes of starting the run, I realized how much I missed my bike. I had spent almost eight hours on the bike, I was accustomed to it; it had become a part of me. Running felt strange, wrong. I had to exert so much more energy to move, and I was much slower. Running felt unproductive, inefficient. Frustration set in, and for the first time in this entire journey, I contemplated quitting.

A guy started running alongside me and began talking to me, but I wasn't in the mood for chatting. My struggle was clearly written on my face, and although he was trying to help motivate me, I wasn't sure it was working. After a few minutes of running together, his watch alarm beeped—it was time for him to walk for ninety seconds as part of his run/walk marathon strategy. As he left, he said something that struck me deeply. "Make sure you enjoy it; everything is about to be over soon!"

Those words made me realize how close I was to the end. I wasn't running the *next* 26.2 miles of my Ironman journey; I was running the *last* 26.2 miles of it. After fourteen months of training, losing eighty-eight pounds, completing two full marathons, a half Ironman, logging thousands of miles of training, and overcoming three injuries, this was it. I had glided through the 2.4 miles of the swim as expected, worked much harder on the 112-mile bike course than I had anticipated, but now I was on the final stage. The grueling run began to feel like a comfortable jog; I started feeling light on my feet, motivated, and even my knees felt great. I was ready to conquer the marathon!

The day grew hotter, and there was no ocean breeze on the run course. To combat the heat, I began drinking lots of water to stay hydrated. Consequently, I needed to make frequent stops at the portable toilets, costing me time. However, I decided it was better to play it safe and lose a few minutes with the stops than risk dehydration in the heat. Things were going well; I completed the first of three laps in one hour and fifty minutes and was feeling strong. I saw my family, high-fived the kids, and doubled down on my water-drinking strategy. At every aid station, I would stop at the bathroom, then grab a water bottle to drink while running to the next aid station. I even decided to pick up my pace, at least for the first part of the second lap, but something unusual started happening toward the end of the second half.

I felt strong, surprisingly rested, and ready to run, but I was having difficulty focusing. It was strange. I started feeling dizzy. I managed to finish the second lap in about two hours, but I wasn't feeling well anymore. I stopped again at my family, hugged them. My daughter looked at me as I approached and yelled, "Run, Dad, run!" Running became more challenging at that point, but it wasn't just a physical challenge. I wanted to run; I had the physical capability to do so, but I couldn't muster the focus. Things started to get tough.

I let Jai know that the last lap would be particularly difficult. I kissed her and forced myself to run a few meters so my children wouldn't worry about me. Once out of their sight, I started walking again, and once again, someone joined me. He asked, "So, is this your second or third lap?"

Without thinking, I replied, "It's my third, but I'm not sure I can make it."

He looked at me and said, "You are well past the point of quitting; I'm sure you will make it." He seemed more confident than I was.

I continued with my water strategy, but things were deteriorating. The next four miles took me one hour and thirty minutes. I wasn't walking; I was dragging myself, and not in a straight line.

During the race briefing, the director had warned us to pay close attention to the course because in previous years, athletes had become disoriented to the point of completing the race, crossing the finish line, and celebrating, only to discover minutes later that they had only completed two laps of the run. Some people even continued running beyond the third lap, believing they hadn't finished. I felt myself approaching that dangerous zone of exhaustion.

I decided to revisit the *Seven Shades of Blue* technique to help regain focus. However, it didn't work; I couldn't concentrate on anything, and an imaginary book was not the easiest thing to focus on. As night fell and the temperature quickly dropped, the streetlights came on. For part of the run, those streetlights are all I can remember. I would fixate on one light, exerting effort to maintain focus on that spot and walk as straight as possible toward it. Once I reached one light, I'd move on to the next and repeat the process. This "firefly strategy" helped me keep moving, carrying me forward for what seemed like yards or miles—time was difficult to gauge at that point.

I tried to distract myself by counting the shades of green in the trees along the course, but in the darkness, they all appeared the same. I have vague memories of nearly fainting; details are hazy, but I distinctly recall several people passing me and shouting, "778, you're doing great!" Of course, I wasn't doing great; it was evident not only from my expression but also from the way I walked, drank water, and ate. I probably appeared intoxicated, and every step became increasingly difficult.

Once again, another runner joined me. I recall little of what he said, except that he was from the army. Cozumel wasn't his first Ironman, and he too was struggling to maintain focus. His concentration had waned, and at that point, he was simply trying to hold himself together to finish the race. He mentioned being certain he was low on sodium, a dangerous condition called hyponatremia, that he had experienced before. Eventually, we parted ways, and I can't recall how it happened—perhaps I was zigzagging too much between the light poles.

If my body was slow, my mind was worse. Just when I thought I wouldn't make it, I began to understand the symptoms the army runner had described. I was experiencing the same lack of focus, difficulty concentrating, and dizziness. However, unlike him, I had sodium in my pocket.

I took a couple of salt pills, and the effect was almost magical. I began to feel significantly better; it was as if I had awoken from a terrible dream. The reason behind my dizzy spells became clear: I had been drinking excessive amounts of water to stay hydrated in the heat, but I hadn't increased my salt intake accordingly. Consequently, all that water had diluted the minerals in my body, causing me to feel faint. It was time to double down on the salt strategy. I took a couple more salt pills, and the improvement was dramatic. The dizziness vanished, my focus returned, and with just four miles left, I was back in the race!

I picked up the pace from a walk, and before I knew it, I was running again—feeling strong and, more importantly, clear-headed. The final three miles of the 140.6-mile journey felt like a sprint, and at that stage in the race, it was. I began passing several athletes; most of them had overtaken me earlier, and they were taken aback to see me in such high spirits. Instead of hearing the usual motivational lines like "You're doing great," people cheered as I passed them, celebrating with shouts of "Way to go!" and "Go get that medal for us!" It was my time then to encourage the ones that were struggling, paying back all the encouragement that I got when I was the one struggling. An Ironman is a race in which everyone cheers and supports each other. For the vast majority, it is not about winning the race, but being better than you were before. It is a race against your own limits, not others.

After a long day—fifteen hours and forty-one minutes, to be exact—it was time for me to hear the phrase I had believed impossible for thirty-seven years: "Acyr Luz, you are an Ironman!"

Whenever I had imagined crossing that finish line, I had pictured myself exhausted, barely walking, and in tears. Reality was quite the opposite; I felt strong, sprinting, and euphoric—it was an incredible feeling. I received my well-deserved medal and finisher's shirt, and it was time to celebrate with my family, who had been there supporting me throughout the entire day and the entire fourteen months of preparation.

For the official finisher picture, I insisted that my wife and kids join me. I wore the official finisher shirt, and without thinking, I took the medal and placed it around my wife's neck. Perhaps it was because she had supported me throughout my entire transformation journey, or because I knew how exhausted she must have been looking after a seven-year-old and a two-year-old all day, or maybe it was because she remained so beautiful even after such a grueling day. Most likely, it was all of these reasons combined. This accomplishment was not just mine; it belonged to our entire Ironfamily.

Crossing IM Cozumel finish line

Official finisher picture with Jai and the kids

With my dad the day after

IM Cozumel medal

IM Cozumel course

Crossing the finish line marked the end of the race, but not the end of my day. The finisher shirt, a long-sleeved one, quickly made me feel unbearably hot right after the finisher picture, so I hastily removed it. Moments later, I started shivering uncontrollably, overwhelmed by an extreme cold. I grabbed a jacket for warmth, only to find myself over-heating again moments later. My body couldn't seem to regulate its temperature. One minute I was chilled to the bone, the next I was sweating profusely. Concerned, my family and I headed to the medical tent near the finish line. They offered me a drink, likely water with salt and sugar, though I wasn't entirely certain. Unfortunately, it didn't alleviate my temperature swings at all.

My family grew increasingly worried, unsure of how to help. We decided to return to the hotel quickly so I could shower and rest. Since our car was parked a bit far, we opted to call a cab. While waiting for it, I sat on a nearby street bench. The constant fluctuations in my body temperature wore me down, leaving me disoriented and utterly exhausted. Eventually, I lay down on the bench and quickly drifted off to sleep, right there in the heart of Cozumel. My body and mind shut down completely.

About fifteen minutes later, the cab arrived, and my wife gently woke me. She was deeply concerned, but I was surprisingly calm. Those brief minutes of sleep seemed to work wonders. In a way I still can't fully explain, it reset my metabolism and stabilized my body temperature. The issues with fluctuating temperatures vanished, and I felt strong and well again. My family was amazed by the transformation; they couldn't believe how quickly I had recovered. Even now, I'm not entirely sure what transpired during that power nap, but it brought balance back to my body.

Upon arriving at the hotel, everyone else was thoroughly exhausted, but I was buzzing with excitement and readiness to celebrate. However, my family lacked the energy for festivities; it was time for them to rest and recover.

The following day, despite the immense effort of completing the Ironman, I woke up early, as I always do. Slowly opening my eyes, I pondered whether everything I had experienced was real or some wild dream. When I attempted to get out of bed, my legs promptly answered any lingering doubts—they reminded me with a lot of soreness of the 140.6 miles of the Ironman. It hurt, but it also felt incredibly satisfying.

The day began with an outpouring of messages from my family back in Brazil, all closely following my journey. Calls from my mom, sister, brother, in-laws, and friends expressed their joy for my accomplishment, each asking the same question: "How are your legs today?" I fielded that question numerous times throughout the day. Initially, my legs felt like they weighed a hundred pounds each and were understandably sore, though nothing compared to how I felt after my first marathon. As I moved about, the lactic acid that had built up during the race seemed to dissipate, and by the time I was receiving calls and messages, my legs were in surprisingly decent shape.

However, to convince everyone, I decided to take a picture—jumping with both legs—to show them. With my daughter beside me and the breathtaking Cozumel sunset in the background, my wife captured a photo that perfectly encapsulated that moment in our lives: we were ready for whatever came next!

Jumping as high as Sophia less than 24 hours after completing the Ironman

December 1, 2014, marked my debut as an Ironman, a day that stood out not just for my family but also professionally, as I began my role as a partner at the firm where I'd dedicated years of hard work. It seemed more than coincidence; it felt like fate affirming my belief. I didn't have to choose between a successful career *or* a healthy life. Instead, prioritizing my health, family, and well-being allowed everything else to fall into place seamlessly throughout my professional journey.

"What's next after completing an Ironman?" was the question I heard most frequently. My immediate response: "Recovery." I meticulously planned a month-long recuperation period, focusing on gentle swim sessions and avoiding running or biking to let my body heal. While muscle soreness dissipated quickly, a lingering discomfort in my knee, especially noticeable descending stairs, persisted. It felt like a loose needle jabbing inside at certain angles and pressures.

Despite initially overlooking the issue, a visit to a sports medicine doctor confirmed my suspicions were valid. Despite feeling no pain during the Ironman itself, multiple knee injuries were detected in the subsequent MRI. The prescribed remedy: rest, ice, and targeted strengthening exercises.

What was intended as a one-month recovery stretched into three, during which I concentrated on swimming and Pilates. Family joined us for the holidays, enjoying a serene white Christmas in Pennsylvania. The highlight of my exercise during this period was leisurely strolls amidst the dazzling Christmas lights at Longwood Gardens, a cherished tradition.

Family visiting from Brazil for Christmas

Everything unfolded rapidly. Embracing endurance sports transformed me completely. Contrary to expectations, dedicating myself to training not only enhanced my professional life but also fostered a healthier lifestyle within my family. They too embraced training and healthy eating, and eagerly awaited race days. Admittedly, my wife wished races started later—5 a.m. wakeups weren't her forte, and I couldn't blame her.

Many cautioned I was progressing too swiftly, advising a slower transformation process. Initially, I should focus solely on running, with a half marathon distance deemed sufficient for long runs in the first year. Following this, I was counseled to complete a couple of full marathons before transitioning to triathlons, beginning with shorter distances, and eventually tackling half Ironman races before contemplating a full Ironman. This phased approach typically spanned three to five years, which was vastly different from my accelerated timeline.

Living in Chadds Ford, Pennsylvania, afforded me an uncommon luxury: a mere thirty-minute commute to Wilmington, Delaware, where my consulting work was centered. Unlike the norm of predawn Monday flights to unknown destinations, late-night work through Thursday, and weekend returns, my local project facilitated a focused training regimen. This contrasted sharply with the logistical hurdles posed by constant travel—airports, fluctuating time zones, and the impracticality of transporting bikes and indoor trainers.

Moreover, delaying an Ironman for three years seemed excessive given life's unpredictability. Potential relocations, career changes, illness, or disruptive weather could derail long-term plans. Consequently, vacations, social events, and personal indulgences took a back seat during training. It seemed more manageable to commit intensely for one year than to sustain such sacrifices over several.

Some cautioned that an incremental approach would have allowed more learning and better preparation. Yet, reflecting on my journey, I'm grateful for diving in headfirst. The accelerated pace made it unpredictable, intense, and ultimately fulfilling. The subsequent recovery period provided clarity on the profound changes—beyond physical transformation, it clarified priorities: balancing family, career, health, and social life.

Completing Cozumel fulfilled a major goal, though I couldn't shake the feeling I could have finished faster. Should I pursue a second Ironman to improve my time? While speed is enticing, the allure of greater distances—the exploration, enjoyment, and mental enrichment—held greater appeal. Endurance lies more in the mind than in sheer physicality.

During this time, I stumbled upon the Ultraman, an ultra-distance triathlon in Hawaii—6.2-mile swim, 261.4-mile bike ride, and 52.4-mile run. Its daunting challenge fascinated me, akin to the allure of Ironman the year prior. When I broached the idea with my wife, her response was emphatic, albeit humorous: "Sign up, and I'll ask for a divorce!" Beneath her jest lay a genuine need for respite—I too recognized the necessity for a break. My body needed recovery, particularly my knees, and I harbored other postponed dreams.

Thus, it was time to return to those dreams, including further education, after a transformative journey into endurance sports.

CHAPTER 14

THE FARM

"Live as if you were to die tomorrow,
learn as if you were to live forever."
—*Mahatma Gandhi, Indian social activist*

2014 TO 2017

Pausing a rising career to go back to school was not an easy decision. To do so, the experience had to be worth it, not only for me but also for my family. Moving again had to be worth it for my wife and kids too. I didn't need to do much research. Growing up listening to stories from my grandfather about a faraway place that, by fate or luck, he had the privilege to study at, my target was set.

With 84 Nobel Prizes, 162 Olympic gold medals, and an annual GDP impact of about 3 trillion dollars through companies such as Google, HP, Nike, GAP, and thirty-nine thousand other companies created by its alumni, Stanford University—the engine of the technology revolution—is a global reference from any perspective: science, sports, and business. As a comparison, Brazil, my home country, with a population of 215 million people and a lot of natural resources, has a GDP of 1.7 trillion USD, 40 Olympic gold medals, and doesn't have a single Nobel Laureate. With manicured gardens, impressive redwood and palm trees, hundreds of art sculptures and monuments, dozens of fields and stadiums, including an 84,000-seat stadium that even hosted Brazil's national team matches in the 1994 FIFA World Cup, Stanford's astonishing campus with over 8,000 acres in the heart of Silicon Valley is also known as "The Farm."

The acceptance rate of 3.9 percent was not encouraging for someone with an undergrad GPA of 2.67, nor were the discussions I had with people around me when I mentioned that I was interested in pursuing a higher degree at Stanford. Disbelief was written on people's faces. One of the senior partners I discussed this with was direct. "Look, the chances of getting in are extremely low. If you want to move to California, we can help you find a good project there, and then you can transfer." I discussed with my career counselor that I might need some time off and asked if the firm would support me financially. His dismissive answer was, "If you get accepted, come and talk to me again." The challenging admissions process and people's disbelief only made things more interesting.

I could not go back in time to change how seriously I took the first years of undergrad, so the only chance I had was to offset the fifteen-year-old low GPA with something academically strong that was much more recent. The best option was to excel on the admissions exam, also known as the GMAT, a four-hour long standardized test used by business schools to level the application process. Not being used to tests like this and living away from math and English books for many years made the whole process hard. I studied for many nights and weekends and did countless practice tests, but I was struggling to break through the published average score for the master's program I was pursuing: seven hundred points, which was equivalent to being in the top 10 percent of test-takers globally.

The exam has two main sections, math, and English. I was hitting the maximum score in the math section but seeing huge swings in the English section. It was inconsistent, and even after several months of studies, I could never beat the score I got in the English section of my first exam. Something wasn't right. Had I just been lucky on my first exam? I didn't accept that easy answer, and one day, I started to investigate what could have happened. Maybe I had taken the first exam at a different time of day. I was quite sure I also did the first exam in the morning, but I decided to double-check. I grabbed my laptop, looked back at my calendar, and confirmed that I had taken the first exam at about the same time I had taken the last practice exams. I was feeling hopeless. Then, I noticed something different on my calendar on the day of my first exam.

There was a flight scheduled for that night from New York to Rio de Janeiro. I asked my wife, "Do you remember that flight?" She shook her head. Something was strange, and when I looked at the details, I was flying alone to Rio.

After a few minutes of trying to reconstruct what happened, my wife then remembered. "Oh, this was during the World Cup. I went to Brazil with the kids two weeks before you."

Suddenly, I could make sense of what had happened. I turned to my wife and said, "If the three of you were in Brazil, it means that you were not here when I did the exam."

My wife's facial expression was not happy with my first observation, and she interrupted me. "Okay, genius, so now it is all my fault that your score went down?"

I answered, "No, but if you and the kids were not here for the two weeks leading up to the exam and were not here on the day of the exam, it means that I barely spoke Portuguese during that time."

My wife's upset facial expression started changing to a puzzled one. Then I continued, "It all makes sense now. For that exam, my brain was functioning nearly all the time in English for two weeks; the verbal questions were more natural to me. It was as if English was my first language at that time." From there, it was easy to connect the dots and understand why my verbal scores were higher after a busy day at work and even on an airplane than they were after a good night's sleep and family breakfast. I immediately turned to my wife and said, "Okay, with one week until my next exam, let's switch the language we speak at home. This will be a Portuguese-free home; we only communicate with each other and the kids in English." And what an interesting week that was. Speaking in English with my wife was odd; we spent more time laughing at the situation than saying anything at all. For the kids, it was just the opposite. They learned Portuguese and English at the same time, and they only spoke English at school, so a week without speaking Portuguese was natural.

On the day of the exam, I woke up early, took a nice warm shower, and decided to wear one of my Ironman shirts that reads IRONDAD, with the Ironman M DOT logo on it. As I was preparing some fruits for breakfast, Sophia, who was always one of the last to go to bed and one of the first to wake up, came to help me. We then sat for over an hour, just the two of us, having breakfast and talking about her week at school and making plans for the weekend. She was only eight years old, and it was so delightful to see her native fluency in English. We had a lot of fun; it was a blast. Breakfast was over. With Gabe and Jai still sleeping, it was time for me to get going, but before that, I needed to pick up a snack for the mid-exam break. I looked at the different fruits and bars I had at home and decided, this time, to go with the energy bar that I used during the Ironman. I was ready for the exam.

The exam flew by. I was on a roll. Essay, math, English questions—I felt unstoppable. The Ironman snacks during the break felt good; the taste reminded me of Cozumel, the splendid shades of blue while biking, and the happiness of crossing that finish line after racing for almost sixteen hours. I felt great, but it didn't necessarily mean that the score would be great too. After almost four hours, I clicked the *submit* button, and the system started to process the results. The confidence gave way to apprehension. The computer took endless seconds to publish the results, and many thoughts crossed my mind at that time. Deep inside, I knew I had done well. I had put in the effort, and I was expecting the coveted 700 score. The score came up; I blinked a few times, looked at the screen from different angles, and almost called someone from the testing center to verify what I was seeing: 750! Yes, fifty points above my goal and the course average. I was not just in the top ten percentile but in the top two percentile. The hard work paid off. In a nonscientific way, I like to say that my studies and preparation for the exam brought me to the 700 score that I really wanted, and my "English" breakfast with Sophia gave me an extra fifty points.

A top score and a killer essay about how I had changed to be more present for my family, in which the Ironman brought things to life, in addition to a successful career, gave me a chance to join The Farm, and what I thought was impossible happened. I was accepted into the 2017 class. It was time to move again to our eleventh house since we got married twelve years before. We were going to our ninth city across three different continents. This time, we were moving from a 2,640-square-foot home in Pennsylvania to a 650-square-foot townhome in Palo Alto. It was tiny, two bedrooms and a single bathroom for the four of us, but we loved it.

The kids loved the freedom of living on campus, with friends from all over the world and a lot of safe outdoor space for them to bike, skate, or just play around. Sophia and Gabe quickly teamed up with four other Brazilian kids, and the six of them would hangout together all the time. Some neighbors would refer to them as the Brazilian Mob. The international community made all of us feel at home quickly. With a lot of parks and gardens, Stanford is the perfect place for running and cycling, not to mention the terrific swimming facilities, all served by the sunny California weather. Life on campus was not about the inside of our tiny home but about the outside, the connection with awesome people, and the abundant nature that surrounded the campus.

Gabe with his preferred Stanford shirt

Sophia teaching Mom how to roller skate

Terrific swimming facilities

At the GSB (Graduate School of Business)

Celebrating a birthday at Escondido Village

The west side of the campus faces the Santa Cruz Mountain Range, which creates a natural barrier to cold and humidity from the Pacific Ocean. The mountains are also the perfect place for cycling, offering challenging climbs that cross redwood forests and nature preserves, providing spectacular views and wildlife encounters. On the other side of the mountains, you will find California Highway 1, the coastal road that connects San Francisco to San Diego. Right after moving west, I decided to explore this world-famous scenic route.

The ocean kissing the rugged green coast with countless cliffs creates magnificent views, and the ocean breeze makes it a pleasant ride. However, the traffic passes by at a considerably high speed, so you need to stay alert, which I didn't do.

I was riding on the aero bars, a position where you have less control of the bike, and enjoying the views. I'm not sure where my mind was, probably in a different dimension. I was then surprised by a fast-moving bus that passed inches from my left side. The air blast caused by that road monster made my bike shake a lot. As I was gaining control of the bike, a second bus, nearly tailgating the first one, also passed close to me. This time, the air blast threw me off the road. Luckily, I was going north at that time and ended up in a drainage ditch. It was not bad; things could have been much worse. The other side of the road had sixty- to seventy-foot cliffs. It was a scary moment for sure, but what I could not imagine was that this incident would help shape my experience at Stanford.

Later that week, I had to apply for a competitive entrepreneurship class called Startup Garage. The professors were clear: don't apply with a business idea because people often do everything possible to make their idea work and do not listen to the market when it is time to pivot. Instead, apply it to a real-world problem that you want to resolve. If it is a real problem, there will be a business around it, and the design thinking process used in the class would help shape it. The problem I wanted to resolve? Bike safety! I teamed up with Markus and Nick, who also got interested in the topic, and together we created the RideHappy team.

One of the key principles of design thinking and lean startup is that you need to spend as much time as possible in the field with your future consumers. Interview them, learn about their habits, and join their communities to find insight. Those insights will be key to the startup's success. For us, it meant spending time on the road, cycling, talking to cyclists, joining bike groups, talking to companies such as Strava, Garmin, and Specialized, and discussing bike safety issues with city officials. We learned that a lot of professors and classmates were cyclists, and they all got engaged in our project. Suddenly, a consultant, a banker, and a navy guy were the bike guys, and in every class, a lot of people would stop by our desk to offer help, make relevant connections, give ideas, tell a personal story related to bike safety, or just to say they were rooting for our success.

RideHappy team conducting field research (left) and having
a brainstorming session (right)

The learning experience was unique. We all graduated from the class with honors and built great connections. The professors later asked us to present to a group of Fortune 500 CEOs who were visiting Stanford and invited us to represent the Stanford students in a workshop with professors from the engineering and business schools to review Stanford's curriculum and approach to teaching entrepreneurship. It was great to learn about people's different experiences and points of view. Half of them were passionate about the idea that startups should start with a problem and then find an innovation that would give an edge to resolve it. The other half had the same passion but for the opposite approach: startups should focus on innovation first, then find a business problem to resolve once they have something unique. It was a privilege to experience that and to be able to make a small contribution to such an important topic, all thanks to a scary moment riding on California Highway 1.

Riding California Highway 1

Riding with Jai and Bruna in the Santa Cruz Mountains (Old La Honda Road)

We did not resolve bike safety once and for all, but we all learned a lot in the process. When I started cycling, I thought that roads with bike lanes or big shoulders were the safest ones to ride, but things changed over time. I realized that those roads were normally busy and somewhat stressful to ride on. I learned that the best and safest roads are the small ones that have much fewer cars. Normally the roads that don't even have the yellow center lines are the best; it is a sign that cars seldom drive there, and when they do, you can hear from miles away and be ready when they come, which was also an interesting discovery.

Intuition will tell you to stay as far to the right as possible, so the car has more space to pass you, but I also learned that this is not very smart either. When you are too far to the right, it is harder for the car to see you, you give him too much space in his own lane, and he will often try to squeeze in between you and the center line, instead of crossing the center line to overtake you as they should. Lastly, you have nowhere to go if the car drives too close to you or if somehow you lose your balance just in front of the car.

In all fifty US states, the cyclist had the right to use the lane unless posted otherwise (places like freeways, tunnels, etc.), so use it. I normally ride a couple feet from the sideline with good visible clothes (yellow or red), making sure the cars see me and force them to plan to overtake me crossing the center line. I keep my ears tuned to when the cars approaching from the back are close. I then move to the right myself, widening the space the car had planned to give while passing me. As it is not hard to have the mind wander when riding in beautiful places such as the sequoia trees of the Santa Cruz Mountains or by the Highway 1 coastline, I also got a Garmin Varia radar, a taillight that detects when cars are approaching and emits a sound signal and flashes some lights on the bike computer. I find it helpful. The risks can't be eliminated, but we can all mitigate them.

Over time, I also moved from flat roads to mountains. I love riding in the mountains. My friend Amee, a top cyclist from Kenya, always tried to convince me to go for the mountains. I hesitated for a while, but once I learned how good it was, I never looked back. Most cars avoid the slow, winding roads on the hills, making the ride nicer and safer, but there are many more reasons to go for the hills. The altitude gives us much fresher air, wonderful views, and in many cases, lets us cross the low morning clouds to enjoy a beautiful sunshine-filled day hidden from the valley. Not to mention how good the climbs are for your brain and body. It is what I like to describe as an effortless effort. I'll explain.

When riding on the flat, you need to have a conscious effort to push yourself and fight the instinct to slow down and take it easy. It is a constant fight within your brain, particularly if you are riding alone. On the climbs, this fight is not against yourself, it is against every foot of elevation gain, and the brain knows that. The brain prepares your body for it. Effortless doses of endorphins, also known as "nature's morphine," are dumped on your system, and you feel like you can ride to the moon. As you conquer the climb, loads of serotonin, the "happy chemical," will join the party and keep you moving. When reaching the top of the mountain, a special guest will be waiting.

The magnificent views from the hilltop and knowing that it is only downhill back home, boost the production of dopamine, also known as the "feel-good hormone" or the "pleasure molecule." Lastly, the rush of adrenaline from the fast downhill will make you alert and ready for anything in life. Not by chance every cyclist that I know loves the hills.

Biking with Amee on Canāda Road, working hard to keep up with her.

Cycling helped me get to know the region I had moved to, allowed me to spend quality time in nature, stay active and fit, and enabled a fantastic academic experience, not to mention the social connections it created, especially because I also joined the Stanford Triathlon Team, which included students from all seven Stanford schools. As part of the team, I had the opportunity to race the US Nationals, but the cost to travel with the whole family on a student budget was too high, and the alternative to travel with the team meant that I had to travel alone, without my family.

I'm sure traveling with the team would have been a lot of fun. Jai even encouraged me to do it, but would it help me with the main objective that made me start with triathlon in the first place? My family was the inspiration to start it all. Letting triathlon distance myself from Jai and the kids didn't feel right, and in the end, despite a strong desire to experience a Nationals championship, I decided not to participate.

Entrepreneurship was one of the main reasons I chose Stanford, and it didn't disappoint me. I learned a lot and loved the experience, but the personal development classes, which I gave little credit to before joining Stanford, were the most impactful for me: leadership classes, public speaking classes, design thinking classes, and even acting classes. Yes, I dared to join acting and loved it. My wife could not believe the day she came to see me on the stage as part of *Four Dogs and a Bone*, a classic play written by John Patrick Shanley. She was shocked. The class was shocked. They even nominated me for the best new actor award after the play. Acting was awesome, but the most impactful of them all was Interpersonal Dynamics, also known as touchy-feely.

Fifteen people sitting in a circle facing each other for several hours in a row, with no predefined agenda, goal, or leadership, just letting the discussion flow. The awkward silence would eventually turn into an unstructured conversation that would morph into a deep discussion that could get heated at times. Throughout the session, people provided feedback to one another on their behaviors, attitudes, and points of view. People often opened up about their personal challenges, shared the ghosts from the past that still haunted them, shared fears and insecurities, and inevitably, they would become vulnerable in front of the whole group. Things could get emotional, and tears were common in the sessions. I joined the class with an open mind and was engaged in all the discussions, but it was hard for me to be emotional in any of the discussions. First of all, I see myself as a rational and pragmatic person, but I believe the main reason that it was hard to get too angry, sad, or excited was because of my swimming routine.

I'd swim for an hour in the beautiful fifty-meter pool over lunch, when the pool had very few people. For me, swimming is always a bit hard in the beginning. With so many things to do, my mind just goes to many places at once, and the time passes so slowly. It is common for me to look at the watch and see that ten minutes have passed. After swimming for another period, I'd look again, and only five more minutes have passed. I have to fight the temptation to cut the workout short. Then, somehow, my thoughts started to get more organized. I start to notice the sound of my breathing, strong and steady. I stop thinking about time, and when I look at the watch again, fifty minutes have passed. And I feel so relaxed. It's hard for any emotion from those discussions to surpass the joy felt after each swim. But the class was designed to take you out of your comfort zone, and it eventually worked.

The last days of class were held in a hotel away from the campus. They were three intense days, locked in a poorly lit room with lots of discussions and not much break, as we would have breakfast, lunch, and dinner together and even share our bedrooms with a colleague from the group. The worst part? No swimming. I could feel the difference. My patience was much lower, the discussions were more heated, and at a certain point, a topic that brought almost the whole class to tears also got to me. It was the first time, right on the last day of class, that I could connect emotionally with almost everyone in the class. The experience was great, but the best part was that not everyone was on the same vibe.

One of the members interrupted the discussion and bluntly said, "I'm extremely bored. I think this is all a waste of time. I don't see why all of you are emotional about something that is not that important." He was probably right. He was probably just being rational, but the cold-water shower that he tried to give the group had no effect. No one cared about what he said. I think that, for the first time, I was not the rational one in the room. I could clearly understand the words he was saying, but they didn't speak to me; they didn't mean anything to me. What a unique opportunity to be on the other side and really feel how many people around me probably felt. The person who immediately came to my mind was my mom.

Growing up, we used to say that my mom had a soft heart. She was very forgiving and would get emotional easily. She would even joke, saying that her heart was made of butter. When things got tough with my dad's bankruptcy, their divorce, and the challenges of raising teenage kids, she had a tough time coping with everything. When things get stressful, I become more rational, a cold problem solver, but my mom does the opposite; she wears her emotions on her sleeve. We could not be more different. All the things I'd tell her to do to resolve the problems just fell on deaf ears, which frustrated me a lot, and I'm sure frustrated her as well. For one moment, in that hotel far away from the campus and from swimming, I could feel what my mom felt many times talking to the son who, according to her, always gave her tough love. What a blessing. Nobody goes through a university such as Stanford and leaves as the same person they entered. The year flew by quickly but made a profound impact on how I see and interact with the world.

With my mom then ...   *... and now*

After being accepted at Stanford, I went back and negotiated with my boss a package that would help financially during the course, in exchange for a commitment to stay with the company for a certain period after graduation. The agreement significantly reduced the risk for my family and allowed all of us to have an incredible year. However, on the other hand, going back to the same company didn't feel exciting. I took less risk than I wanted to, and I'm sure a lot of this had to do with the hardship of living through my dad's bankruptcy and seeing my family as I knew it back then disappear. I turned that difficult moment into something positive for my life, but others had a much harder time doing that, and I didn't want my wife and kids to experience something similar. Going back to the same company also made it easier for me to take the lead role with the kids and house stuff, so my wife could pursue her own grad school and restart her career after fifteen years of moving around the globe. In the end, it worked out well for the family, and something else sparked my interest.

Family at graduation: Tata, my niece Bia, Marcelo, Mom, Jai, Gabe, me, Sophia, and Dad.

CHAPTER 15

FINDING ULTRA

"The difference between ordinary and extraordinary
is that little extra."
—*Jimmy Johnson, American football coach*

2018 TO 2019

Listening to music was strictly forbidden in the Ironman races, so when I started training for Cozumel, I ditched the headset, as I thought it was important to train as close as possible to the way I'd race. But occasionally, I'd use the time running to listen to a podcast or an audiobook. Just by luck, I stumbled on a book about Ultra. I didn't know much about the book or the author, but as the app had recommended it, I decided to give it a try. To my surprise, the author, Rich Roll, was a Stanford alum, and the way he described the campus and life at Stanford really drew me to the book, which is well written and tells Rich's incredible life story. This includes a mind-blowing triathlon race that had caught my attention a few years earlier. This time, Rich's words brought it to life, and after completing my third Ironman, I decided to pursue a much bigger challenge: the Ultraman World Championship.

Swim 6.2 miles in the open ocean off the coast of Hawaii, bike 261.5 miles across the Big Island's volcanoes, and run 52.4 miles across the lava fields of Mauna Kea, a massive volcano that is the tallest mountain in the world when measuring from its underwater base. Everything sounded challenging, scary, and inhuman. I loved it. My wife didn't. To make things more complicated, each competitor needs their own crew to support them during the race. Of course, I asked her to be my crew, along with the kids. After some time and a little persistence, she agreed, but it would be a one-and-done kind of thing. Or better yet, it had to be two and done because, before racing in Hawaii, I had to qualify. There are not many Ultraman races in the world, and at that time, only Ultraman Canada was accepting applications. Yes, Ultraman is an invitation-only race, and one needs to apply to try to get an invitation.

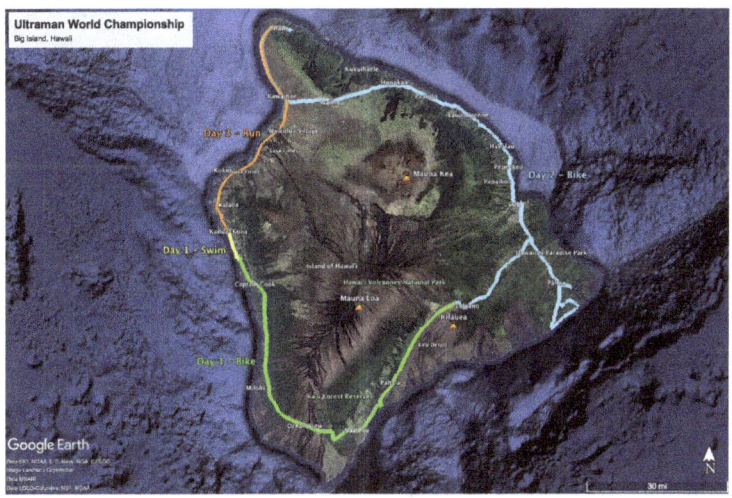

Ultraman World Championship Course

To apply, you have to provide your endurance background, list your recent races, list your longest races and their times, and you have to have completed an Ironman in the prior eighteen months. There are a lot of questions about swimming, and you must provide evidence that

that you are an experienced open-water swimmer. In addition, you also need provide information on how you support the sport and the community you live in. The first part of the application is to make sure that everyone who enters the race will be safe, and the second part is to make sure that the people who will eventually join the race will live up to the spirit of the race, defined by three Hawaiian words: *aloha* (love), *kokua* (help), and *ohana* (family).

In October 2018, I got invited to join Ultraman Canada, which would happen over the upcoming summer in Penticton, British Columbia. It was now time to form the crew.

My wife had reluctantly agreed to crew for me, but she got excited when I shared with her that the race would be in a wine region and that she could spend most of the day exploring the wineries while I rode and ran. She just needed to meet me once every four hours to refill my water bottles and nutrition. I have to say, her excitement waned when she learned that the 6.2-mile swim, for which she would have to kayak to support me, would happen in the Okanagan Lake, home of the Ogopogo, the Canadian version of the Loch Ness Monster. The kids, on the other hand, got excited about the possibility of seeing a lake monster.

In the end, my wife's excitement about the wineries overcame her concern about the mythical monster. I also talked to my sister Tata, who, like my wife, is also a wine lover, and she got excited to join us in Penticton. My friend Yon, with whom I had raced two marathons and a half Ironman, also decided to join us, completing the team that would be enjoying the wineries while I raced. They'd meet me every four hours. Little did we know about the Ultraman.

With three Ironman races in the bag, I was confident when I signed up for Ultraman Canada. The distances were much longer, but the race was split over three days, with a time limit of twelve hours for each day. Day one included swimming 6.2 miles and riding 90 miles. Day two was just riding, 171.5 miles, and day three was just running, just running a lot—52.6 miles. A couple of months after being accepted, my confidence shook a bit. The organizers published the bike course, and it included eight thousand feet of elevation gain on day two, with references to a steep section called "The Wall."

I loved the climbs, and since moving to California, all my training had been in the mountains, but there were no time cutoffs in training. In Canada, I'd have to ride 171.5 miles with eight thousand feet of elevation and a wall in the middle in less than twelve hours, meaning an average speed above fourteen miles per hour. I had never completed a ride in the mountains with an average above twelve miles per hour, and my rides were much shorter.

My confidence continued to deteriorate as the race approached. Work picked up significantly; I had to step in to recover a project, and my training time got cut to less than half of what I had planned. With that, I had to go more aggressive with the little time I had, increasing training volume much faster than I should have, which brought back some old knee injuries that I had to manage in the last two months of training. Things were not looking good, and a week before the race, I discussed with my wife whether I should pull out. In the end, she thought the experience would be worth it, no matter what. Maybe the wineries had something to do with that.

Race week arrived, and the breakfast briefing session wiped out the little confidence I still had. There was so much information about crewing, the course, the weather, and more. Everyone in the room was engaged, asking lots of questions, and taking a bunch of notes. Everyone but my crew and me. We arrived a bit late, the kids were hungry, and there was almost no food left when we arrived. My wife had to focus on finding food for them while the session was running. Tata, Yon, and I would look at each other; it was hard to understand who was more lost.

The organizers would explain the leapfrog method for crewing while cycling and emphasize the no-feed zones, especially around The Wall.

They were reviewing the racecourse, which everyone seemed to know well, and how it was being modified because of the wildfires caused by the excessive heat. It all sounded Greek to us. But the worst part was when the athletes were introduced.

Every athlete in that room had an impressive background with many ultra races on their resume. Everyone but me. A common favorite race among the competitors was Badwater, a grueling footrace of 135 miles (217 kilometers) that starts at the bottom of Death Valley at -282 feet of elevation and finishes at Mt. Whitney's summit at 14,505 feet of elevation. Not to mention that the race happens over the summer in the hottest place on planet Earth. Some athletes in the room were doubling down on the Ultraman; they were doing Ultraman Canada that weekend and another similar ultra triathlon the weekend after. My three Ironman races and a couple of marathons felt so small in that room. I finally understood the meaning of "impostor syndrome." I don't know what they saw in my application to invite me to the race. I didn't feel I belonged there at all. But at that point in time, there was just one thing that I could do: race.

To start, a point-to-point 6.2-mile swim in Lake Okanagan. My wife was nervous, as she was responsible for navigation, and there were just no buoys to mark the course. We all entered the lake on one small beach and had to aim at the twin buildings far, far away. Before she had agreed to kayak for me, she had never set foot in a kayak. We had planned to train together on the open-water swim sessions, so she could practice, but the reality was different. The busy schedule allowed us to do one twenty-five-minute session. It was enough for her to learn that she was much faster on the kayak than I was swimming. In addition to the navigation challenge, she also had to manage my nutrition during the whole swim, which we had not practiced at all. Adding more anxiety to a day that had started at 4 a.m., one of the kayak suppliers didn't show up on race day, so the race officials had to scramble at 5:30 a.m. to find fifty backup kayaks, as each athlete has their own kayak support. It caused the start to delay for a long hour. At 6 a.m., we could already get a taste of the heat that was reserved for us throughout the day.

Just before 7 a.m., the swim started. Jai and I got into a good rhythm right off the bat. The water was beautiful, calm, and clear, and there was not a single cloud in the sky; visibility was great. With a steady pace, we could see the twin buildings on the horizon grow bigger as we got closer with each stroke. Things were going smoothly. I could see my wife taking pictures, enjoying the experience, and I was on track to finish at about the same time I had completed the 6.2-mile practice swim in Santa Cruz the month before.

But as I approached the three-hour mark, my performance plummeted, and I started to struggle. I had taken gels during the swim, but they didn't feel great. I wanted something else, something salty, but we didn't have anything salty in the kayak. During training, I never craved salt for obvious reasons—I swam in the ocean—but I had not made that connection until that moment. I dragged myself for the last half hour and managed to complete the swim in three hours and thirty minutes.

Leaving the water, I could see how different my preparation and my crew were from the other athletes. I left the water side by side with an athlete from Spain, and waiting for him outside was a whole team. Someone helped him strip off the wetsuit, while another crew member was passing sunscreen, and a third person would give him food while providing information about the bike course and weather. Waiting for me was Gabe, who was seven years old, in his Speedo. He came out of the water to high-five me and say, "Good job, Dad," then ran back to the water to refresh himself from the heat. Sophia was cheering for me a bit further, close to the tent where I'd change. She was there to point me in the right direction to find where the bike and all the others were after I changed, but I was not feeling well from the swim and needed time to recover.

It took me about forty-five minutes to change, recover, and eat something, but there was a challenge: I could not even look at anything I had planned to eat during the day. All the gels, bars, and blocks looked too sweet; I had no appetite for them. On the other hand, the ham-and-cheese sandwich that my crew prepared for themselves looked delicious. And they were delicious. Luckily for me, they had prepared enough sandwiches that could carry me through the day, and it resolved a big problem for me, but of course, it created a big problem for them—what would they eat? Without many places to buy food along the course and with a lot of concern about leaving the course and struggling to find me afterward, they didn't have much choice but to eat the running bars and blocks I had planned to eat myself. The problem was that those bars and blocks were filled with all kinds of sugar and some with caffeine, which is not a great combination with kids locked in a car. Things were getting messier by the hour.

Recovered from the swim and with a successful plan B for nutrition working, it was time to face the most surprising challenge for a race in Canada: a heatwave. With the temperature reaching 113°F (45°C), the region was suffering from wildfires, which required changes to the bike course. The heat really got to me, especially on the climbs. My crew got ice and started to fill my water bottles with ice first, then added some water to complete it, but it would not last long; in less than an hour, the ice would melt, and it felt like I was drinking hot tea. Concerned with the heat, my crew also put ice on my back, inside my shirt, but I could not even feel it. I slowed down and took it a mile at a time; the good time on the swim allowed me to take it easy, at least for the first sixty miles. Then came the last surprise of the day: a flat tire.

As described at the beginning of the book, I chose a fast tire to have a chance to complete day two within the cutoff time, but the faster tire was less puncture resistant, and I ended up having to pay the price for my choice. My crew was close by when I noticed the flat on day one; I waved, they stopped and pulled out the spare wheel, and in less than five minutes, I was riding again. I asked them to stay close because another flat could mean not finishing the race. The second flat didn't come on day one, and I was able to complete it successfully. But the flat—or better saying, the *flats*—came on day two and got in the way of a particularly challenging bike day, described in the first chapter, "No Easy Day."

Missing the cutoff for day two by eight minutes after overcoming a heatwave, flat tires, and windstorms was hard. Forty percent of the athletes didn't complete that day, including athletes who had completed the race before, others who had completed Badwater, and even athletes who had planned back-to-back Ultraman races. I was the first athlete to miss the cutoff; all the other ones who missed the cutoff were behind me. The last athlete to make the cutoff had done that race a couple of times before and said that that day was the worst by far, that he had completed it an hour slower than his personal best. Considering all the challenges I faced in training and racing, my result was surprisingly positive, but it was hard to have any motivation to wake up at 4 a.m. the next day and run 52.4 miles on hilly terrain for a race that I had been disqualified from already. But the Ultraman was not only about me.

My crew, who learned the hard way what crewing really was and that it had absolutely nothing to do with spending time at wineries, actually enjoyed the first two days of the race. My wife said that it was stressful and exhausting but more interesting than an Ironman race because she was not just a spectator; she was a key part of the race. Ultraman had turned triathlon into a team sport and my family into a team. The team wanted to run, so it was time to pick myself up from the floor, rebuild my motivation, and get ready for the double marathon, so we could at least finish the trip with good memories, but the plan backfired.

Training for Ultraman Canada was challenging; I ramped up the distance too quickly, and I had to battle some knee pain that caused me to cut back on the long runs. My longest run leading up to the race was fifteen miles, probably half of what I needed to have run. The course didn't help either; it was very hilly. I'd have to sprint on the downhills to offset the time lost on the climbs in order to have a chance to complete the run within the cutoff times. At 13.1 miles, I was fourteen minutes below the cutoff time; at 26.2 miles, I was only four minutes. At 39.3 miles, I was within one minute of the cutoff time and had to sprint to get there on time. I then decided to walk for a bit to catch my breath, and that was the end of it. After walking for ten minutes, I tried to restart running, but my legs would just not follow my brain. I kept trying and pushed myself for over two hours. I was trying to reach the final downhill and was hoping I could unlock my legs there, but I was a slow walker, and it never happened. I never reached the last downhill and never restarted running. With forty-four miles and about twenty minutes left, we all decided that it was time to pull out of the race and drive to the finish line so we could at least see some of the athletes complete it successfully.

The outcome was far from what we all wanted, but there were a lot of positive things from the whole experience. Jai enjoyed the kayak experience, everyone enjoyed being part of the team, and my cycling and running performance was way above what we expected, considering all the challenges we faced. Yon's phrase by the end of day two echoed in my head: "After today, I'm convinced you are built for this." We all left with the feeling that we were close, that with the learnings from Canada plus a bit more training, we could complete an Ultraman, so I didn't waste time. Back home, I started to research what Ultraman options were out there, and by a stroke of luck, Ultraman Florida 2020, which was sold out, had just had a cancellation that same week. That spot was meant to be mine; there was just a small issue: the race was happening in six months, so I had to be efficient with my training. But how would I do that?

At that time, I was working with a big tech company in the Bay Area and had subscribed to the employee cycling community and email distribution list. A few days after registering for UM Florida, someone sent an email to the group asking for tips for his first Ironman. I replied with what I thought could help him and then closed my email with an unpretentious question: "Does anyone here have any experience with Ultraman?" To my surprise, there was one: Rob Gray, the 2017 Ultraman World Champion. Rob and I had the chance to have lunch shortly after the email exchange, and I could learn a lot from his experience, especially about running the double marathon. Some of his tips were unconventional.

First, I learned that the training volume per week was more important than the distance of a single day's long run. Then he shared that he normally includes short thirty- to forty-five-second walks during the run, especially at the beginning, to help save the legs for the end. There was the Ultraman world champion, proud of his walk/run strategy, shattering a big paradigm for me, an aspiring ultra-athlete. I always refused to do runs/walks, likely driven by the insecurity of not feeling or being seen as a true runner. Lastly, to my huge surprise, he said that he would not go crazy on a single day's distance; instead, he would start his long run from the top of a mountain and sprint downhill to wear down the quads. Then, he would run a couple more hours on fatigued legs to simulate the end of the double marathon. With that, his long-run sessions were much shorter than the expected distances for such a race. I have to say that my knees would hurt just from thinking of sprinting downhill, but I decided to incorporate it into my training for Ultraman Florida.

The knee injury was my major concern, so I decided to do the downhill session only once and well in advance of the race. That way, if anything happened, I still had time to recover. Six weeks before the race, I drove up Page Mill Road to the highest nearby mountain, which has about seven hundred meters of elevation and six miles of downhill. I had ridden that road many times and knew every inch of it, which helped because no cyclist or driver would expect a runner on that road, so I needed to be extra cautious. Going downhill allowed me to achieve a good pace at a low heart rate, and going fast was actually easier than going slow; I felt a lot less pressure on my knees. The road had some very steep parts that reach a 16 percent grade, and I had planned to walk down those parts. Instead, I learned that I could run them down by lowering my body and shortening my stride. Someone hearing me running down the steep sections could think was a horse running down the hill. The knees were fine, but by the end, my quads were burning! After the downhill, I continued running on some roads that I used to bike on for another twenty miles. This went fine for the most part, but any downhill, even going down a speed bump, would make me feel the burning sensation in my quads.

Ultraman training turned my bike routes into running ones and car routes into cycling ones. I needed to learn new ways to train to cope with the brutal distances. In addition to the tips Rob gave me, a low-heart-rate training method proposed by an unconventional coach, Phil Maffetone, resonated with me. Phil was one of the first people to measure heart rate in athletes and had trained successful ones. But his approach to endurance, which can be found in many of his enjoyable books, goes against the "no pain, no gain" mentality. In fact, the expression he uses is "no pain, no gain, no brain." His approach focuses on training one's body to use stored fat as fuel for endurance instead of sugar. The whole process takes time and discipline, but once done correctly, it enables one to train for long distances without getting injured, and that was exactly what I was looking for. Later in my journey, Rodrigo, a friend and hardcore endurance athlete recommended the book *The Triathlete's Training Bible* by Joel Friel, and it helped a lot as well. The books complemented each other and gave me a deeper understanding of how to train efficiently.

Race week arrived before we realized it, but this time, I felt much more confident. With the same loyal crew, I headed to Florida, feeling confident about what lay ahead. Training had gone well, and no one on the crew expected to spend a minute at a winery. Plus, I had gotten the right bike tires this time. I knew I would not get a third chance, and I felt ready, but a race of this magnitude always reserves surprises, and in Florida, the surprise arose early.

Once again, my wife agreed to be my kayaker, and at 7 a.m., we entered Lake Minneola for the 6.2-mile swim. Things looked okay; I missed the clear water from Canada, and I would choose swimming in a lake with a mythical monster anytime over one filled with gators. To be fair, no gator showed up that morning; the surprise came from the skies. A huge storm entered the area around 8 a.m., bringing a lot of rain and wind. The water became choppy, and the wind made things hard for the kayakers. Jai, who had a pleasant experience in Canada, had to work hard to keep up with me swimming. At the peak of the storm, it was hard to see the buoys, and I had to stop, wait, and wave for Jai while she worked super hard to move the kayak forward. For a moment, I thought the race would be over then, but Jai pulled it off, cursing me with each paddle stroke—I'm sure she was having a blast. Jokes aside, it was a dire situation; some kayakers flipped, and one of them sank, forcing the athlete to quit the race. Jai made it, swore that she would never step into a kayak again, and struggled with tendonitis in her elbow for a couple of years after that day. I still hear about her tendonitis.

Jai kayaking with me on Lake Minneola

Sophia keeping track of the progress

I ended up finishing the swim at the same time as I had done in Canada—three hours and thirty minutes—but in much better shape. After a quick transition, I was rolling on the bike. This time, my crew and I were much better prepared; they had sandwiches for themselves and for me too. We learned that I could not rely only on those running gels and bars. The good time on the swim and the fast transition allowed me to take it easy on the bike; I just wanted to finish day one, preserving myself as much as possible for the next two days, which indeed happened. I finished day one in ten hours and thirty-five minutes, almost an hour and a half before the cutoff. After crossing the finish line, we rushed home for a relaxing Epsom salt bath, to get as much sleep as possible. I knew the next days would be different.

Swimming in Ultraman Florida

Day two started with a different vibe this time; I was there to complete those mind-blowing 171.5 miles in less than twelve hours. Right before the start, I told Yon, "Hey, I'll probably want to start taking electrolytes with caffeine halfway through, but I'll let you know when I feel I need it." Yon nodded; the nutrition plan was set. The day started with some rain, but I didn't care. I was there to ride strong, and that's what I did; from the beginning, no pause, no rest, and no break either. On the downhills, I continued to push, passing forty-five miles per hour. About an hour into the race, I made a quick stop to take off the rain jacket and give it to my crew. With about three hours in, I made another quick stop to apply some oil, as the bike chain was a bit squeaky; the morning rain probably washed away the oil that was there before. Those were the only two stops that day, and they added up to less than five minutes. For the rest of the day, I was riding strong on the hills of Clermont, Florida. Halfway through, I was still feeling strong. In fact, I was feeling stronger than when I started, so I decided to defer the caffeine boost until later in the day; my concern was taking caffeine too soon and overdoing it.

With nine hours of riding at a frenetic pace, I had covered about 135 miles, and at that time, I was confident I would be able to cross the finish line in less than twelve hours. But I started to feel fatigued, so the next time I passed my crew, I slowed down, looked for Yon, and yelled, "Yon, it's time for the caffeine!"

Yon's jaw dropped. Time slowed down; he looked terrified. I got confused, slowed down even more, and suddenly Yon yelled back, "I have been giving you caffeine for the last three hours!" Then, I was the one terrified. Immediately after, Yon said, "I probably should not have told you that."

I nodded and kept riding. The plan to have a caffeine boost to finish day two strong was replaced by the concern of having pushed too hard without realizing it. I then changed my strategy for the last part of day two; I slowed down a bit and biked at a higher cadence to preserve my legs for the double marathon of day three. At eleven hours and forty-four minutes, I crossed the finish line—a relief! Now, I just needed to run a double marathon.

I got disqualified in Canada on the second day for missing the cutoff on the bike, but it was close, and external challenges played a significant role in that. On the other hand, I was not able to complete day three either, and deep inside, I knew it was a much larger failure; I was only able to run thirty-nine miles. I trained more this time, but would it be enough? I trained differently, using downhill training and a run/walk strategy and adapted my body to burn fat instead of sugar. But would all these things really work? To be honest, I was unsure; my confidence level in running is not even close to my confidence with in biking or swimming. But I would not go down without fighting; I was ready to leave everything on that course to cross those 52.4-mile hills in less than twelve hours.

Cycling in Ultraman Florida

Day three started an hour earlier than the other days, to allow all the athletes to cross the finish line in daylight, but that meant one hour less sleep that my crew and I really missed. Everyone was cranky and stressed in the morning. Jai wanted a detailed plan of how much distance I should cover each hour and didn't like my honest answer. "My goal is to cross each half marathon mark within the cutoff times of three, six, nine, and twelve hours." At 5 a.m., she started lecturing me that a goal is different from a plan. I then replied, "My plan is to meet my goals!" Things didn't get any easier after that. Tata then entered the discussion, trying to help, and Jai got more upset because she thought Tata was just protecting her "little brother," me. Gabe and Sophia were fighting for a more comfortable position inside the crammed SUV, and among us was Yon, always calm in the middle of the storm. He would stretch his rusty Italian to try to catch something from the arguments we all had in Portuguese to calm everyone down. At 6 a.m., everything went away; it was time to start the 52.4-mile journey.

The beginning was great; we started before dawn, and the cool temperature made running a pleasure. My legs were stiff in the beginning, but things got better as I warmed up, and my legs didn't feel too bad. After thirty minutes, running actually felt good. Tata joined me for the first miles to check how I was doing, and we enjoyed a beautiful sunrise while running together. Throughout the day, she would rotate with Yon, Jai, and the kids; one at a time would run side by side with me.

Things got a bit hard when we hit the red roads, a mix of sand and red clay that made running slow, and we could really feel the heat. It was a safer road for the kids, so they ran most of it with me, breaking the boredom of being in a slow car the entire day. Gabe would run sideways, crossing his right foot in front of the left, then crossing it behind it, in what he called karaoke running. It was reminding me that I was not going fast. It was fine; it was a day to go long, not fast. I just needed to hit the cutoffs. I crossed the 13.1-mile and the 26.2-mile marks twenty and twenty-seven minutes below the cutoffs; things were looking okay, but they got a bit tense by the thirty-nine-mile mark.

I had slowed down and had only twelve minutes to spare. At that time, I ran past my crew, and they had stopped to talk to Slava, a Russian athlete we met in Canada (her crewmember was the one in the white minivan who gave me water when my crew got lost) who was volunteering in Florida. Right after that point, things changed with my crew. I could feel the stress level had gone up; the tension was stamped on their faces.

I didn't have time to stop; I was sure everyone was concerned with the time, and so was I. At that point, I dropped the run/walk strategy and tried to pick up the pace. The next time I passed my crew, they were all inside the car, gearing up, doing some calculations, looking at the route, or something similar. Sophia was the only one outside to hand me water and food, but she had her back to me and would not respond when I called her. When I approached her, she was crying a lot, and I asked, "What happened, Sophia? Did you fall or something?"

With a lot of frustration and anger, she replied, "No, Dad! I just wanted to run with you, but Yon said that I couldn't because now you need a *real pacer! Dad, I am a real pacer!*"

Oh my God, I had been running for nine straight hours, was under a lot of pressure to complete the remaining distance, and suddenly, I had to deal with the hurt feelings of my twelve-year-old daughter. I said, "Sophia, I know that this is important to you, and I want you to know that you have been an *amazing* pacer, but I just don't have time to talk through this right now. I really need …"

She stormed away, grumbling before I could even finish my sentence. Right after that, Yon joined me and helped me understand what happened. He told me that Slava gave them a hard time. "Are you all doing your job? Are you pushing him enough? He is losing ground and will not make it in time; this is on you! You all gotta push him, drive him; at this point in the race, he can't think anymore. He barely knows where he is right now!" They all got so scared that things got a bit out of control. When I mentioned to Yon that Sophia was crying because of what he had said, he was shocked.

"Oh, did I make her angry? I was just trying to help."

Slava's tough love was good, but the reality was I knew exactly where I was, and despite being exhausted, I was conscious and aware of everything. I was in better shape than my pacers. At forty-six miles, an alligator crossed the road right in front of Yon and me, and don't ask me how, but he didn't even see it. I did. My whole crew—Jai, Sophia, Gabe, Tata, and Yon—joined me for the last mile of that odyssey, so we could cross the finish line together. There was not much time left, and the closer we got to the finish line, the more people joined us to help overcome the fatigue and the pain of 320 miles of swimming, biking, and running.

Dozens of people surrounded us and started singing, counting, roaring, *"You got this!"* Time was running out. Ten minutes left, nine, eight … The finish line is magic; it pulls you. The pain and fatigue started to fade away, and I started to increase the pace gradually. With seven minutes left, the finish line appeared on the horizon; it was sprint time! As I accelerated, the crowd started to dissipate—some high-fiving me, others shouting encouraging words, everyone with unbelievable positive energy. As we approached the finish line, they were all gone, letting my crew and me cross the finish line together, celebrating what fewer than one thousand people in the world have done—completing an Ultraman. And with a whole five minutes to spare!

All of us crossing the finish line at Ultraman Canada

CHAPTER 16

GO BIG. BIG ISLAND.

"Success is not final; failure is not fatal:
It is the courage to continue that counts."
—*Sir Winston Churchill, English statesman, prime minister*

2022

Waking up to the sound of the ocean is always a blessing, even at 4 a.m. I walked to the balcony and took a peek at Kamakahonu Beach and the Kailua Pier. Things were still quiet. I could hear the small waves breaking and feel the cool breeze. Everything was so peaceful, but things were about to change. I checked my phone, and there was an email from the person who was supposed to meet me in one hour to escort me on the 6.2-mile swim from Kailua-Kona to Keauhou Bay. I hesitated to open it; it couldn't be good news. And it wasn't: *"Acyr, I woke up sick and will not be able to meet you this morning. I'm sorry."* Not the best start for day one of the Ultraman World Championship.

After four years of training, I was physically and mentally ready for the race, but there would not be a race without a kayaker. Tata, who was still asleep on the nearby bed, always got seasick; she was not up for the job. Jai, who was sleeping with the kids in another room because Sophia was recovering from the flu, was not up for it either. After her traumatic experience on the lake in Florida, there was no way she would paddle on the open ocean. I had to rely on the race directors, who had helped me find the first kayaker, to help me find a replacement. I texted Sheryl, one of the race directors, who replied almost immediately, *"Working on it."* Time started to pass quickly. Before I realized it, it was already 5 a.m. The pier was filling with athletes, crewmembers, kayaks, and kayakers—everyone but my kayaker. Sheryl was there, working on a million things to start the race at 6:30 a.m. She had to check in all the athletes, answer everyone's questions, get the sound ready, and clear the area. It is not an easy task to put on a race, and she had one more challenge: helping me find a kayaker.

View of the Kailua Pier. Swimmers start on the left side of the pier, kayakers on the right side of it

Time continued to pass quickly, and every time I checked with her, she had the same answer: "Working on it." Ten minutes before the start, the race announcer began asking all athletes to go to the water. Everyone did, except me. I was still searching for a kayaker. Sheryl called me: "I found someone; she will be here shortly." Five minutes before the start, all the athletes were in the water and ready, except for me, who was still holding my nutrition bag to give to my kayaker. She finally showed up. I handed her the bag, and she looked at it, then at me. "What is this?"

I replied, "This is my nutrition. I'm supposed to drink a bottle an hour plus the gels ..."

She interrupted me. "Oh, do I have to give you anything out there?"

At that point, it was clear to me that giving her more details would make it even worse. I then said, "Don't worry, I'll tell you what I need out there. We just need to meet each other a couple of hundred yards from here. I leave from the pier, and you leave from the beach."

She said, "That should be easy; you are a tall guy ..."

It was my turn to interrupt her. "Wait, I'll be in the water. You will not see me, just my cap. Memorize my number. I'll yell it, and you do the same, okay?" She nodded while I rushed to the water. The cannon blasted as I was entering the water. It was time to start a long day.

While preparing for the race, I listened to some podcasts, especially from athletes who had completed the Ultraman in Hawaii. One that really caught my attention was from a Japanese athlete, whose advice was, *"Do not underestimate the swim!"* Although swimming is my strongest of the three sports, I took his advice to heart and trained a lot for it. I was swimming over thirty miles per month in the months leading up to the race, more than double what I had trained for the other Ultraman races. But even after so much training, I made a rookie mistake. Two days before the race, I went to shop for new swim goggles and got convinced to use trendy new goggles that seemed more like a mask, as they gave better visibility in open water. I trained once with them, things were fine, and I decided to wear them on race day.

With a long, sunny day ahead of me, Tata insisted that I put on a lot of sunscreen, which I'm normally not good at doing. The good intention backfired, and the sunscreen extravaganza didn't allow the mask to seal properly on my face, causing the mask to leak water. I have used many goggles before, and water leakage was not a new problem. I just needed to use the hand that is outside the water during a stroke to quickly open the top side of the goggle to remove the water and keep swimming. I had done that thousands of times, but the simple technique didn't work with the mask-type goggles. As it was in one piece, the water would always fall to the bottom of the mask, and opening the top part didn't help. I ended up having to stop halfway through a stroke to use the hand that was underwater to open the bottom part of the mask. Shame on me for falling for the new shiny toy. At that time, I considered changing the mask goggles for the old goggles that were in the bag I had handed over to the kayaker. But where was my kayaker?

Within a few minutes, I reached the area where the kayaks were waiting for the swimmers and started searching for mine, but without success. I'd yell my number to every kayak that passed by, but there were no signs of my kayaker. I looked around; everyone was pairing with their kayaker, and mine was nowhere to be found. In the heat of the moment, I had to make a call and decided to keep swimming, hoping that my kayaker would eventually find me. Without someone to help me navigate, I used other kayakers as a reference and kept going. Five, ten, fifteen minutes passed, and no news on my kayak. At that point, I was certain I'd have to swim it solo. Once in a while, a Jet Ski monitoring the race would pass by. I'd yell my number and ask for help to find my kayaker. The guy on the Jet Ski would nod and take off. My main concern at that point was that the race officials would pull me from the water since I could not be swimming alone.

As in any swim practice, the first ten minutes were long and a bit stressful, but then my mind somehow adjusted, got in rhythm, and even the nasty mask goggles sealed properly to my face—no more water leakage. I somehow entered an alpha state of mind, and everything just flowed naturally, stress-free, even alone in the middle of the Pacific Ocean. The swimmers spread out, and as it was harder to see the kayaker in front, I started to use the mountain on the tip of the island as a reference and kept swimming. After forty-five minutes, I was mentally ready to complete the swim without any support, but then I saw a double kayak working hard to catch up to me. Yes, finally, there was my kayaker—or rather, my kayakers. The person I met right before the swim start was not very experienced on the ocean, so after talking to me, she went searching for another good soul to join her on the kayak so she would not go alone. It took time for her to find someone, which is why she was not at the meeting point when I passed. The kayakers brought a lot of relief, and I decided to focus on the time. My main worry was that currents were expected to pick up around 9:30 a.m., and I wanted to have passed the 5.5-mile mark by then, so I'd be in a protected area. But the ocean had different plans for that morning.

After ninety minutes, I had covered almost half of the course. I was on a roll, but the ocean became choppy, and the swell grew bigger. The ups and downs on the ocean, combined with the difficulties of breathing in choppy water, caused me to swallow a lot of seawater. The navigation challenges, because the waves got in the way of seeing the surroundings, made me feel sick, but I kept pushing. I needed to cross the 5.5-mile mark before 9:30 a.m. The nausea increased by the minute. I slowed down, but it was too late; my stomach had flipped by then.

At a certain point, I stopped and signaled my crew to stay while I tried to take control of my body, but it was useless. I started throwing up while swimming in choppy water. What a horrible experience. And it was bad. I managed to hold on to the kayak, but things got worse. I flipped inside out. The waves would shake the kayak in all directions, and it would bounce on me while I held on not to drown. The kayakers got scared, and their immediate reaction was to call for help. While still pulling myself together, I convinced them not to do it. I was not ready to give up that fight.

In distress, struggling to stay afloat in the middle of the ocean with tons of predigested food around me, sharks were the first thing that came to mind when I recovered my senses. I did my homework and knew that I was swimming in tiger shark territory. In fact, that area is one of the key destinations for pregnant tiger sharks, and we were at the end of the season. In other words, they were there. My belief is that sharks are less likely to go after a swimmer who is in full control of his "mission." There are plenty of easier and tastier options for the shark out there. Have you ever heard of shark attacks happening in a triathlon race? Me neither. But on the other hand, a floating guy feeling sick with a lot of smelly, tasty food around seems way more interesting to the apex predator of the ocean, who knows from miles away when a potential prey is in trouble, like I was. I needed to get moving, and I needed to do it fast, before I was the one asking to be pulled out of the race. The window to cross the 5.5-mile mark before the current turn was closing.

I resumed swimming. My kayakers looked at me, curious to see how I'd react in the water. After a few strokes, I looked at them and shouted, "It was just like a hangover!"

They started to laugh and celebrate. "Let's do this!"

I picked up the pace and wanted to make up for the lost time, but things didn't go as planned. I could not come to terms with my stomach. The nausea came back several times, and I'd try to manage as much as I could. Many times, I'd not stop swimming; instead, I'd turn and swim looking backward, which would allow me to throw up but continue to make progress. Then I'd turn to the front again once I was done. Other times, the nausea would be way too strong, and I had to hold on to the kayak to avoid drowning.

The frequent stops and the reduced pace killed my chance to cross the 5.5-mile mark before the currents picked up. At 9:30 a.m., I was still at the four-mile mark, and the last 2.2 miles were a drag. To beat the current, I'd have to push hard on an empty stomach and dehydrated body. My heart rate would climb quickly, and with that, the nausea would kick in, and throwing up was inevitable. While recovering from the sickness, the current would push me a few yards down, leading me to question if I'd ever get out of that nightmare cycle. But I did. After three hours of throwing up and retching, I was able to complete the 6.2-mile swim in four hours and twenty-two minutes. To my absolute surprise, I was the twenty-first out of the water out of forty competitors, but I was not in any physical state to compete in anything at that point.

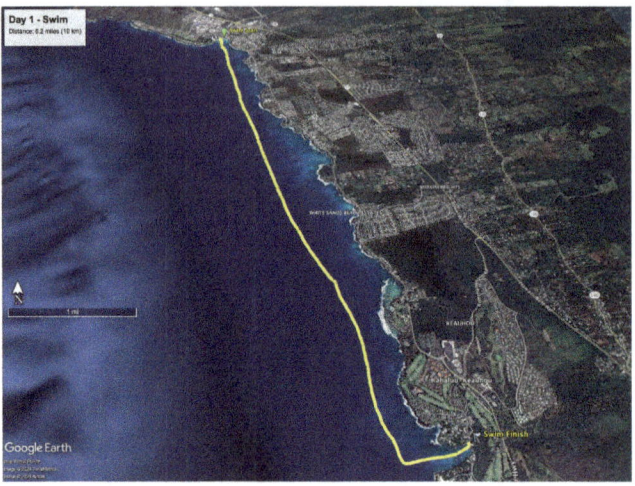

Day one swim course

I swam until I could touch the rocks at the bottom with my hands. Solid ground, finally. I looked up and saw Tata waiting for me with a towel. I stopped swimming and stood up, but my legs were weak. I could not hold my balance and fell back into the shallow water. I stood up again, but the uneven terrain and strong currents were not much help, and I fell once again. The rocks that seconds earlier provided relief were now another obstacle. Tata stepped into the water to help me not fall for the third time. Tata got scared. It was written on her face: *"Game over."* Or at least that's what I read. That's what I really wanted at that point. I was so weak and dizzy, I just wanted that agony to stop.

Tata hauled what was left of me to the transition area to meet Jai and the kids, who were carrying a gallon of fresh water to help me rinse off the salt water and get going, but I could not get on the bike. I could barely balance standing on my feet. Still undecided on what to do, I went to the bathroom nearby for a shower, hoping it could reset my physical condition. Looking in the mirror, I could see the damage from the swim. I was pale, beaten down; it was not good. It looked like I had been sick for days. In New York, I craved carbs because my body desperately needed sugar to keep the pace I was running the marathon. In Cozumel, I craved salty food because my body needed sodium to keep up with the water I was drinking. This time, there was only one thing that I was badly craving: an intravenous fluid injection.

Quitting was the most sensible thing to do. What was left of every muscle in my body urged me to quit. I felt nauseated just thinking about eating anything. But I could not let everyone down. How would I look my kids in the eye after quitting? And all the effort Jai put into the preparation? Tata had traveled across half of the world to support me. I could not go down without fighting. I knew I would never forgive myself if I quit. Fifteen minutes after completing the worst swim ever, I hopped on the bike to face the merciless course ahead. It started with a steep one-hour climb on the side of Mauna Loa, the first of two volcanoes that I had to climb that day. It was hard to do it right off the swim exit, with no time to recover.

The first challenge was the burning sensation in my feet; more than an indication of heat, it is an indication of dehydration. I was not able to drink or eat anything after the swim. Just looking at water would make me sick. I almost fell in the first hundred yards, and to top it all off, the sun was pounding on my head. At 11 a.m. the temperature was already 104°F (40°C). At that point, I didn't believe I'd make it to the top of Kilauea before 6:30 p.m., but I was ready to continue fighting. Slowly but steadily, I climbed that first steep hill. My crew was tremendous; they never gave up on me. I would see them in every corner; they were almost walking side by side with me as I climbed the hill. They were trying to give me different food and drinks, but nothing would work.

Based on the previous Ultraman experience, they gave me a sandwich. But this time it was made of a gluten-free sliced bread that was not toasted. The thing was inedible. Someone in the crew had the idea to try a soda. It helped—the sugar, caffeine, gas—it all helped stabilize my stomach. I got a second one, then started to move to real food (not that gluten-free sandwich), and a little bit at a time, I started to recover. By the end of that hour of steep climb, I had to face almost three hours of a less steep climb. Everything was challenging. The long transition time and the slow start on the bike made me fall from twenty-first to thirty-first, but after climbing for four hours, I started to have hopes that I could eventually close the day in less than twelve hours.

After all that climbing, I just took off on the downhill; it was my chance to make up for the lost time, and in twenty minutes, I was back at sea level. The adrenaline rush gave me the confidence I needed to face the last section of the course, one last long climb, from sea level to the crater of Kilauea, twenty-five miles straight up, with no break for the lungs or for the legs.

Right at the beginning of the climb, three athletes passed me, and shortly after that, Doug, a race official who was monitoring the bike course on a red motorcycle, came by. He slowed down, looked at his watch, looked at me, and said, "To make it, you need to catch those guys." I nodded, he nodded then took off. I put together the last piece of energy I had and started an uphill chase of those three cyclists who had just passed me. Every time I'd pass my crew, I'd give them something that I was wearing or that was on my bike that was not strictly mandatory, just to save weight and make the climb marginally better. Tata started laughing when I gave her my gloves, the wrapper of some food I had eaten, the bike radar that weighed less than an ounce, and more. Every ounce counted. After about an hour, I passed the first one and kept chasing the other two. Doug would pass by several times; most times, he would just close his fist and swing his arm, telling me I could do it. If I was not looking great, he would slow down, ride his motorcycle alongside me, and help boost my energy. "Keep these wheels rolling. You will get them. Push!"

Another hour later, I passed the second rider, and the third rider was in sight. Doug would slow down by my side, point at the guy, and yell, "Catch him!" Things were looking good. It took me another thirty minutes, but I eventually got to the third rider and prepared to pass him. But the engine, also known as legs, started to fail. The dehydration and depleted muscles started to scream.

The right upper quad started to cramp up. I started to push harder with the left leg, letting the right one recover. It worked for a bit, but then the left upper quad started to cramp up too. I'd rest that and push with the right leg, then both upper quads started to cramp up. I got off the saddle and started to ride standing, positioning myself as much in the front as possible to use distinct parts of the muscles. This also worked for a bit, but then both my legs would cramp up. I almost fell.

The struggles continued. I'd rotate position, and alternate which leg I pushed harder, anything to overcome the cramps, and with that, the third rider started to pull away from me. My crew and Doug would stay close to me, trying to lift me from the struggles. I'd slow down a bit, let myself recover from the cramps, then push to catch the third rider. I never gave up, but my legs did.

The third rider crossed the finish line with sixty seconds to spare, and I missed it by 180 seconds. What a hard defeat to swallow.

So much training, so much preparation. My crew and I were extremely invested in the race emotionally, and I felt more ready than ever. Everything was gone in three minutes. A single stop during the swim to recover from nausea was longer than three minutes, and I had dozens of stops. I wasted more than three minutes just searching for my kayaker. No matter how much I had trained for the race, I felt nothing would get me ready to face what I faced on the water that day, especially because I had never gotten seasick in my life. Not to mention that I had never cramped while riding either. In the end, I convinced myself that my learning cycle before I could complete the Ultraman World Championship was not complete yet; there was more to learn before I could finish that race.

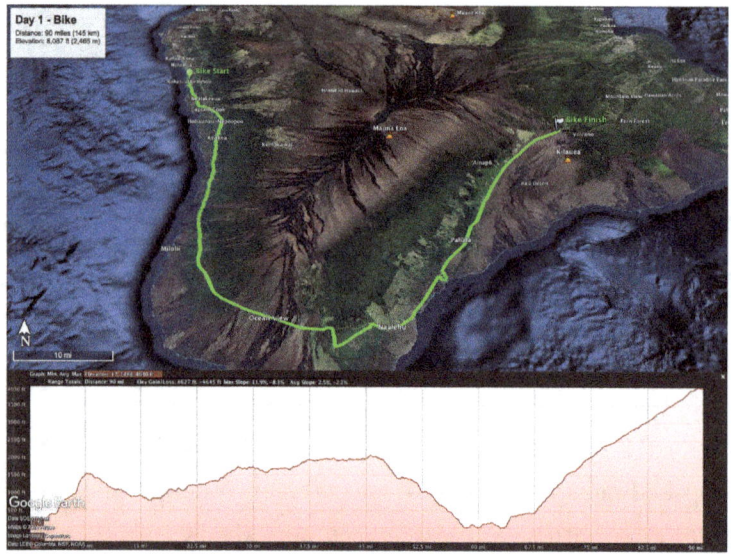

Day one bike course and elevation chart

After missing the cutoff by three minutes, the race organizers, other athletes, and my crew wanted me to continue racing. It was hard, especially because I had an unpleasant experience back in Canada when I did that. I was too exhausted to make any decision, so I decided to go to the hotel, take some rest, and decide in the morning. The warm night at the hotel and the support from my crew helped me decide to line up for day two. Once again, I woke up at 4 a.m., geared up, pumped the bike tires, and headed to a cold starting line at four thousand feet of elevation. Physically, I felt good, but my motivation was nonexistent. The gun went off, and we all started descending the twenty-five miles from Kilauea to Keaau. It felt strange. I felt so slow. I could see all the athletes taking off, and even pushing hard on my crank would not help, I could not keep up with the group. It didn't feel right. The more we went down, the wider the gap became, and in twenty minutes, I had lost sight of everyone. Then, suddenly, I got a flat tire. I called my crew, who were still at the hotel, and said, "The race is over, I got a flat." When I changed it, there was no puncture in the tire; the flat happened from the rim bumping on the corner of the road, which normally happens when the tires have low pressure. I had put the right pressure in that morning, but maybe there was a small leak that I didn't realize. But at that point, I must confess that I was happy to call off the race; my motivation to ride 171.5 miles and to run 52.4 miles didn't exist. When I met my crew, we packed up and went to a black sand beach nearby to enjoy the day. We just didn't know it was a nudist beach, but that is a story for a different book.

CHAPTER 17

〰〰〰〰〰

UNFINISHED BUSINESS

"Life is not measured by the number of breaths we take, but by the moments that take our breath away."
—*Vicky Corona, American author*

2023

My Ultraman story could not finish on that three-minute failure. There was too much training and emotional investment to leave behind. The discussion at home was not easy. Back in 2018, we had agreed that the Ultraman would be a one-and-done kind of thing. Four years and three Ultraman races later, I had not achieved what I had planned. After a lot of discussions and negotiations, my wife agreed to do it one last time. There would not be a third chance in Kona. With that in mind, I decided to get as much help as possible to cross that finish line, and the best person I could think of to help me was the same person who had helped me complete Ultraman Florida three years earlier, Rob Gray. He was clearly knowledgeable, had a good understanding of my family and business commitments, and had an efficient approach to training, which is what I really needed.

Another thing that I did differently was to load the year with prep races to experiment as closely to reality as possible, and nothing was better than a real race to do that.

The Escape Alcatraz Triathlon was the first prep race, and what a race it was! The 2023 edition was special because the 2022–23 winter had been the snowiest season ever documented in California, and the melted snow from the Sierra Nevada filled the rivers, resulting in massive currents of about three miles per hour (2.5 knots) that we had to cross while swimming from Alcatraz to the shore. It was like crossing a fast river. The race was memorable.

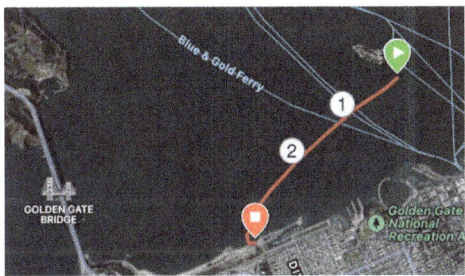

Alcatraz swim heading to the shore, but the current pulled toward the Golden Gate Bridge

Finisher picture of Escape Alcatraz

A few months later, I did the half Ironman in Santa Cruz, and it was great. I had done this race six years earlier, but after so much training, I managed to complete it an hour faster. I was flying! The last prep race was Ironman California, a full-distance Ironman used as training, during which I suffered a lot, but it helped me tremendously.

The race started with a swim in the American River, a main destination during the Gold Rush, and finished on the Sacramento River. Still under the influence of the snowiest winter ever, their flows were strong and pushed hard during the swim. While most people swam close to the riverbank, I positioned myself in the middle of the river, where the flow was stronger, and swam as if I didn't have to ride 112 miles and run 26.2

miles afterward. My ambitious goal was to complete the swim in less than one hour. I did it in forty-five minutes and felt great at the end. Jai and the kids almost missed me exiting the water because I was too fast.

I quickly hopped on the bike and was determined to complete the 112 miles in less than six hours, which would give me an average speed greater than 18.6 miles per hour. I was on track to finish in less than five and a half hours until the last quarter of the course, when it started to rain heavily. No one ever goes out to train in a weather like that, so there were a lot of first-time experiences in the race. I had to relearn how to use the brakes. With such a heavy rain, I had to pull the brake levers strong first just to clear the water from the brake pads, which were not working at all. After that first strong pull, I'd release the levers then quickly pull them again, braking normally, almost as if it was a dry day. But if I would not do the pull, release, then pull again approach, the brakes would just not work. The roads became slippery, and a lot of athletes crashed.

Luckily, I managed to complete the 112 miles unharmed and, as a bonus, in less than six hours. Things were going well, and I had planned to take it easy on the marathon, as I only had four weeks until the Ultraman race. The problem is a marathon never takes it easy on you.

The first ten miles went by quickly, but then I started to feel fatigue in my legs. I continued to push, but with every mile, running became harder; my legs were getting stiff. By mile thirteen, I felt as if I had already run a full marathon, and the rain came back heavy, flooding everything, creating rivers on the road. I started to walk and run, but running was extremely difficult. I had the strength to start running but struggled to keep going; each footfall became increasingly painful. I ended up having to walk most of the second half of the marathon under heavy rain, crossing many flooded areas, and as night fell, the temperature plummeted.

The medical tents started to fill with people suffering from hypothermia, but because of my great times in the swim and bike, I managed to cross the finish line before facing hypothermia myself. Despite the terrible performance in the run, I still achieved my best Ironman time by over an hour, but that was not the goal of the race.

Special help on preparing for the race   *Racing Ironman California
(Sacramento)*

The main objective of the Ironman was to test my preparation for the Ultraman, and I failed miserably. How would I run 52.4 miles four weeks from then if I could barely run 13.1 miles well in Sacramento?

It kept me up at night, and I wrote to Rob asking for help. The next day, we had a call to try to understand what had just happened. I had trained nineteen miles back-to-back days, and in my peak week, I had run over forty-four miles. How could I not run more than 13.1 miles that day? We discussed nutrition, weather, and rain, but nothing really added up to an answer. We hung up, and I continued to ponder what could have happened. The feeling of stiff legs was similar to what I had experienced during the run at Ultraman Canada four years earlier and during the Napa Valley Marathon two years before that. I started to search for any similarities among the three events to find something that would lead me to an answer, but nothing stood out for me during the day.

I woke up in the middle of the night and started to study my training logs and courses. Suddenly, everything made sense. I could clearly see the pattern: downhill training was killing me. Yes, what I believed was a secret weapon to shortcut training was backfiring, as I needed a long time to recover from it. I had done downhill training ten days before Ironman California and had not recovered from it, so with thirteen miles, my legs shut down. For the Napa Valley Marathon, I had done downhill training four weeks before the race, but even that time was not enough to recover, and my legs shut down after eighteen miles. Ultraman Canada happened before I even knew that downhill training existed, but the course had a lot of downhill sections that certainly wore down my quads, causing my legs to shut down after forty miles. The only time that downhill training seemed to have worked well for me was before Ultraman Florida, when I had done it six weeks before the race. There were five-and-half weeks between my last downhill training and the start of Ultraman Hawaii.

That same night, I sent an email with my findings to Rob, who was surprised, but it all made sense. We developed a recovery plan to be ready for the double marathon: no downhill training, elliptical training to save the legs, and massage to accelerate recovery, and we also developed a strategy for the race itself. Among other things, the strategy called for starting the double marathon with heavier but more cushioned shoes, then switching to the shoes I had trained in for all those years after the marathon mark. Nothing scares runners more than messing with their shoes. I was concerned and unconvinced about switching shoes halfway through.

Life is full of ironies. Failing in that last Ironman California marathon was the best thing that could have happened to me that night. Rob had planned a weekly downhill training session until close to the Ultraman race. If I had not failed in Sacramento, I would not have a chance in Hawaii. Getting disqualified the year before for being three minutes over after fighting seasickness for three hours felt horrible and somewhat unfair, but believe it or not, it was also the best thing that could have happened to me in that race.

I didn't know it back then, but I was 100 percent set to fail in the double marathon. I had done my last thirty-one-mile run with eight miles of steep downhill just three weeks before that race. Two days before race day, I was still feeling my quads burning. When the pain went away, I thought I was ready, but now I know I was not; I needed three more weeks to recover. It was hard to rebuild myself after failing for a reason that was not under my control; I had no way to know that I could even get seasick swimming. But it would have been an even harder task to rebuild myself because I could not complete the double marathon, even though I had trained as hard as I could to do so.

I'm not sure I'd have had the strength to motivate my family and restart the journey. I often tell people that after many years in consulting, the best promotion was the one to partner that I didn't get; it helped me see things that were wrong in my life and gave me the energy to do something about it. Making peace with the past is probably one of the best ways to move forward. That painful, wet, and cold marathon from Ironman California helped me finally make peace with what happened in Hawaii the year before. I was ready to go back, this time to finish it!

Going back to the Big Island within twelve months gave us a chance to enjoy what didn't work out well the last time. We all got flu and COVID shots ahead of time; none of us got sick. We rented the right car to visit the Mauna Kea summit, got lucky with night snorkeling among the majestic manta rays, and had fun watching dolphins and sea turtles on the beach. We even managed to squeeze in a college visit for Sophia to the University of Hawaii at Mānoa. Everything was going well this time around. The only point of concern was the swell; the forecast called for large waves hitting the Kona shore on Friday, day one of the race. People in town were sure that the swim portion of the race would be canceled, but at the race briefing on Thursday, the directors reinforced that the swim would proceed and emphasized a crucial rule: "Keep the island on your left; the rest will be fine." Jokes aside, I was relieved to hear that—I hadn't trained for another year just to have the swim canceled upon arrival.

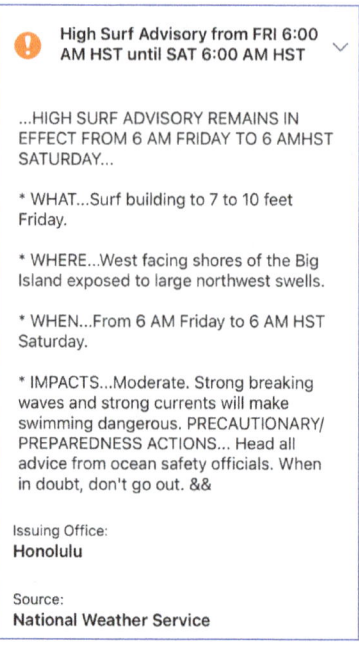

High surf advisory

Once again, it was time to wake up at 4 a.m. and check the empty Kailua pier from the balcony. The breeze was the same as the year before, but the waves were not. We could hear it. A high surf advisory was issued for the area: "Strong breaking waves from 7 to 10 feet and strong currents would make swimming dangerous. When in doubt, don't go out." Fortunately, I was not in doubt. Right at 4 a.m., upon reading the severe weather alert, I took an anti-nausea medicine; I knew I'd need it soon. By 5 a.m., almost ready and without sunscreen on my face this time, I received a text message from Jeff, my kayaker. Déjà vu? I cautiously opened the message that read, "Just parked. Coming over." What a relief!

At 5:30 a.m., we met by the pier, checked in, and prepared ourselves for the long, challenging swim ahead. Jeff, an avid surfer familiar with that part of the island, wasn't overly concerned about the big waves we were about to face. He was more preoccupied with a huge case of FOMO (fear of missing out) for not surfing the largest waves he had seen since moving to Kona a few years before.

Team Luz the day before

Team Luz ready for action

Right before entering the water, I picked up a second anti-nausea pill. Jai questioned it. "Are you sure you are going to take two pills? You've trained only with one pill before." Yes, but the San Francisco Aquatic Park didn't have ten-foot waves. I didn't overthink, broke the pill, took half of it, and said, "Let's split the difference. I'll go with a pill and a half!"

At 6:30 a.m., the cannon blasted, and I was back in the water. No issues finding Jeff at our meeting point, and we quickly got into a good rhythm. The swell was huge, and seeing the island with my head above water was not an easy task. Jeff stayed close enough on my right side, and I trusted he was keeping the island to our left. Stroke by stroke, I made progress.

Once again, things got choppy around three miles, and even with anti-nausea medicine, I started to feel a bit queasy. I stopped, took off my cap, adjusted my goggles, and drank a bottle of soda, something that

Rob had recommended. I was glad to have taken more than one pill. It worked; I had no nausea this time. The big waves brought mighty currents, much worse than the year before. It was not an easy swim out there, but I managed well. At 5.9 miles, we reached a turning buoy to enter Keauhou Bay. In my mind, I thought I had finished the swim, but not quite. Jeff read my mind, and as soon as we turned, he said, "Look, the current is unusually strong here now because of the waves. You'll have to push harder to bring this home." He was right; those last 0.3 miles were extremely tough, and I had to dig deep to keep the pace. I did it. At three hours and fifty minutes, I completed a tough swim safely.

Swim start —
Photo by Matthew D'Avella

Swimming with Jeff —
Photo by Matthew D'Avella

Leaving the water, Gabe stopped me and asked, "Dad, did you see the manta rays? They were swimming by your side the whole time!" I was so focused on overcoming the current that I hadn't even seen anything. I rushed to the transition area; it was time to get ready to bike ninety miles to the top of the Kilauea volcano.

No shower this time; in less than four minutes, I was already on my bike, facing the hills to first climb Mauna Loa and then Kilauea. The hot temperature and headwind made it feel like I was in an air fryer at times, especially when passing the Ka'u Desert. The final twenty-five-mile straight climb to the crater seemed like a bird cemetery; I had to maneuver around the poor little creatures that couldn't survive the excessive heat. The ride was not great. I was feeling drowsy, probably from the anti-nausea medicine, but was able to cross the finish line with about twenty minutes to spare. Good thing I didn't take two anti-nausea pills that morning.

We then headed to our Airbnb to recover for the next day. We were all so tired, and the house seemed isolated, so we decided to leave the bikes and most of the gear in the car. I arrived exhausted, and within minutes, I was in bed. I slept so deeply that night that I woke up completely refreshed, ready for the 171.5 miles ahead. But before that, I had to get my bike and pump up the tires. Leaving the bike outside seemed like a bad idea, so I put on a jacket and braved the chilly morning at four thousand feet of altitude. I ran to the car, grabbed the bike, then hurried back into the warmth of the house to pump up the tires. As I quickly entered, carrying my bike, I noticed something strange. All I could see were balloons. Party balloons. A lot of things suddenly made sense. Those warm/cold/warm changes reminded me of our time living in Minnesota—a beautiful place, but I don't miss one of the coldest winters on the planet a bit.

A funny memory surfaced of picking up helium-filled balloons at a party shop. They looked great inside the shop, but as soon as we crossed into the cold outside, they would deflate, only to reinflate once inside the warm car. The process repeated itself as we moved the balloons from the car to the house. The light bulb went off as to why I was so slow going down the Kilauea descent the year before and even got a flat tire.

My bike spent the night inside a warm hotel, and in the morning, I pumped up the tires inside the same warm hotel. But the temperature outside was about 30°F cooler. Of course, I wasn't going downhill with the tires at 110 psi anymore—maybe 80 psi? Who knows? I immediately took my bike back outside, released all the air from both tires, and pumped them up with cold outside air. I was finally ready for the Kilauea descent, and what a descent it was!

We all lined up based on our day one finish times. I was in thirteenth place out of twenty-one athletes. At 6:30 a.m., the gun went off—it was time to ride, or better yet, time to fly. It was a dry morning, a rare day in Kilauea's history. I wanted to take advantage of the downhill and the cool morning temperature to cover as much ground as possible before the heat and hills arrived. From the start, I pushed hard, got into the aerobars, and stayed there for nearly the entire descent. The tires performed perfectly; I had never felt so fast. In no time, I had passed half of the people ahead of me. Speed is seductive—the adrenaline, the wind, the sense of freedom—it's reinvigorating.

After dropping me off at the starting line, Jai rushed back home to pick up Tata and the kids, who were still getting ready. They began driving the twenty-five-mile descent after all the athletes had started. They soon started passing athletes one by one, but there was no sign of me. Eventually, they passed some athletes from the top group on day one, but still no sign of me. They were all worried; their first thought was that I had crashed or fallen off the road, and they had passed me without noticing. They tried to locate me using the cell phone tracker, but most of the course had no cell signal, so they continued on. Almost at the bottom of the mountain, they caught up with me. My wife said I was in second place. I could see their shocked faces. I loved it and pushed even harder!

I had been lucky to have a dry downhill from the volcano, which is rare. I was given a chance to gain a lot of time early in the race, and I took it. My average heart rate on that downhill stretch was higher than on any other part of the bike or run courses, even higher than on the uphill stretches. It just wasn't higher than my average heart rate during the swim—those waves and currents left their mark!

The north side of the Big Island is also known as the wet side of the island. We were lucky that the downhill was dry, but right at the bottom of the mountain, heavy rain awaited us. The conditions were similar to those four weeks before in Sacramento: flooded areas and slippery turns, but with one complication. My cycling goggles were completely foggy. I couldn't see a thing. Without them, I couldn't look forward; the speed turned the raindrops into tiny sharp needles that hurt my eyes. The only choice was to ride looking down. Unlike Sacramento, the heavy rain didn't concern me too much. I didn't take my foot off the gas; I knew I still had a long way to go. The experience of riding, braking, and turning on those conditions was still fresh in my mind, and the massive adrenaline rush from the downhill helped me keep going fast. Later, I learned that at least three athletes crashed on that slippery part of the race; luckily, I made it through safely.

The wet side of the island is beautiful, with massive trees, parts of it resembling a rainforest. What a contrast from the arid landscape of the dry side of the island. Another benefit of the rain was that it kept the temperature low—Northern California cold, perfect for working out. But the rain eventually passed, and the heat came. At that point, I had covered over sixty miles, and I knew I would complete the race with plenty of time to spare.

Steve King, the voice of Ultraman, is a special person who follows along with the athletes, always positioning himself where he can narrate the race in real-time, making all of us—athletes and crew members—feel special. He keeps track of everyone's performance, history, and personal situation, weaving them into his announcements. It is always a pleasure to see him on the course and, of course, at the finish line. I passed him about halfway through the race, and his eyes widened, and his jaw dropped. For once, I can say I left the official Ultraman announcer speechless; he was not ready to see me that early in the race. In fact, after the race, I asked him if my observations were correct, and he confirmed them all. I was on a roll. My crew was on a roll! Every time I passed them, I could feel the energy; that van was a party.

Mauna Kea arrived, and I took it easy climbing with the sun at its peak. At the top, I could feel the strong wind coming from the other side of the mountain, which meant that going downhill to the dry side of the island would not be easy. The strong crosswinds and heavy traffic made the Mauna Kea descent dangerous. Right before starting to descend, I took a pack of salt pills, and I think the extra awareness helped; at least I finished that challenging downhill in one piece. Arriving at the bottom, the blast of heat immediately made me miss the wet side of the island and, of course, made me worry about running the day after. Like in Florida in 2020, I increased the cadence and reduced the power in the last miles; it was time to prepare my legs for the final test: the double marathon. With over an hour to spare, I crossed the finish line of the Ultraman World Championship feeling great, and my crew was in a state of grace. We have done many races together; this was our fourth Ultraman race, but I had never seen my wife, Tata, and especially the kids so happy. Sophia would yell, "Dad, there is still daylight; this is unbelievable!" Gabe wanted to go to a swimming pool nearby to celebrate. This time the feeling was different; we didn't just finish it, we crushed it!

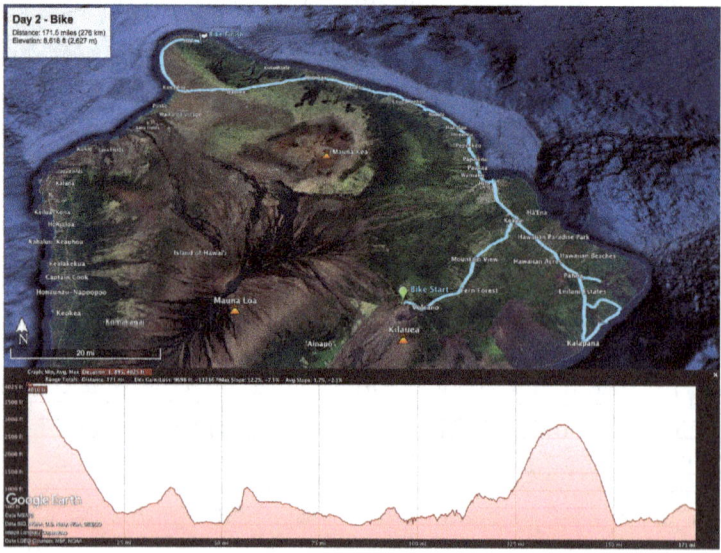

Day two bike course and elevation chart

Cycling in Ultraman World Championship — Photo by Matthew D'Avella

Finishing day two strong — Photo by Matthew D'Avella

Once again, a beautiful sunrise marked the beginning of the double marathon, blessing another long day. From the start, I could tell it would be a sweltering day as well. The first hours went well; this time, we aimed for eleven hours, leaving one hour as buffer. I used the same nine-minute run, one-minute walk strategy to preserve my legs. As recommended by Rob, I started the race with the cushioned shoes and planned to complete the race in them; switching seemed risky. The first 13.1 miles passed quickly, and I completed it in just over two and a half hours, but the temperature was already above 95°F. I had to change my entire nutrition plan. I switched from a calorie-heavy drink to one rich in electrolytes. My crew started stopping at gas stations along the way to get ice cream to replace bars and gels and to refill ice; I needed a lot of it. At every stop, I loaded my hat with ice, put it on, and ran with the ice melting on my head, dripping icy water on my face and body.

Start of day three — Photo by Matthew D'Avella

Shortly after the half marathon mark, Tata, who was running with me, turned to me and with a shocked expression on her face shouted, "Oh, we are screwed." She then pointed to my shirt. When I looked down, my new white shirt was red. Bloody red. The heat and sweat wore off the anti-chafing, and both my nipples were bleeding a lot. I had not felt anything. My mind was too focused on overcoming the heat and the hills ahead. I still had thirty-nine miles to go and knew there were no flats until the end.

In Hawaii, you're either going uphill, which slows the pace, or downhill, which strains the quads, and the hot headwind makes everything harder. It felt like being in a convection oven, especially when crossing Mauna Kea's lava fields. I managed to stick to the plan for the first marathon and completed it in five hours and twenty-five minutes, but things were looking grim. Fatigue in my legs was starting to show, and the temperature was above 104°F (40°C). My crew knew I needed extra support. Sophia put loud music to boost our motivation, but it seemed like it was a playlist of a single song. Every time I passed the car, I could hear AC/DC's "Highway to Hell." We couldn't argue that the song wasn't fitting for the circumstances.

Around the forty-mile mark, things got tough. The hilly course, the brutal temperatures, the burning headwinds. I still had almost four hours left, but things were incredibly challenging. Jai, Tata, Sol, and Gabe took turns running with me, but my legs were nearly spent. They questioned several times if I should change my shoes, but I hesitated; an injury would ruin the race immediately. My right quad started to bother me a lot; I could feel it was weak. Raising my leg from the ground was becoming an arduous job, so I naturally shortened my stride, slowing down even more. Things were not going well, and my mind was not helping either.

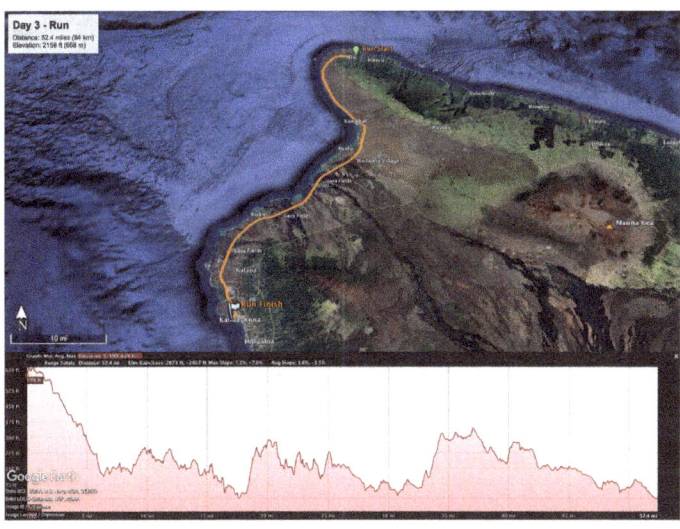

Day three run course and elevation chart – no flats

It started to go places that would not help me. The extreme heat reminded me of Ultraman Canada. I started to feel down. Defeated. It was a familiar feeling, similar to the way I felt missing the day two cutoff in Canada, similar to the way I felt the year before, having missed the cutoff of day one in Hawaii by three minutes. The disappointment and guilt of letting everyone down were vivid in my mind, more than ever. I lacked the strength to shut down those thoughts and decided to walk. My crew was there in the double marathon in Canada and knew I could not walk more than three minutes straight, otherwise the lactic acid in my legs would build up, and I would not be able to run again. They pushed me to keep running, and when they saw it was too hard, they insisted that I change shoes.

In a desperate move, I finally agreed to change them. What a blessing it was. The lighter shoes rejuvenated my legs, and I was able to start running again. Around the same time, Suzy, a race official, stopped by to check on me. She gave my crew a lot of tips, offered to pace me, and kept checking on my progress frequently. A bit later, another race official approached on a red motorcycle; it was Doug, the same kind soul who had escorted me on the Kilauea climb the year before. His expression this time conveyed confidence. Doug and Suzy teamed up, rotating to check on my crew and me, offering guidance, directions, tips, but most importantly, smiles, support, and friendship.

With two hours left in the race, a blessing from the skies occurred—the dry side of the island saw a lot of unexpected rain, which cooled the temperature down. It felt fantastic. I was able to increase my pace, which was back to almost the same pace I started with. Tata, Jai, Gabe, and Sophia continued to rotate, running different stretches with me, pacing me, carrying my food, my water, and more importantly, my spirit. They were unbelievable!

With less than one mile to go, there was a big downhill. Finally. As I prepared myself to increase the pace and take the gravity advantage, Suzy stopped me and said, "You should walk down that hill. I have seen many people cramp up when running down it. You don't want that." No, I certainly didn't want to drag myself for the last mile, but thanks to my crew and angels that appeared along the way, I did not need to.

Sweaty, bloody, and exhausted, but happy conquering
yet another hill with some of the lava fields on the back.
Photo captured by Suzy while passing my crew on a support stop.

With eleven hours and thirty-nine minutes on the clock, Jai, Sophia, Gabe, Tata, and I crossed the finish line together—as a team, as family. We accomplished the unthinkable; together, we completed one of the toughest races in the world, the Ultraman World Championship. Crossing the finish line was a mixture of happiness, excitement, pride, exhaustion, and relief.

Getting the medal was wonderful, but in some ways, it felt unfair that I was the only one receiving it. I would not have done so without my crew. But the award ceremony the day after reserved yet another special surprise.

Race directors, volunteers, athletes, crewmembers, and families all got together the next day for the award ceremony. It was an opportunity to see all the remarkable people with whom we had shared the last days, and exchange pictures, stories, and gratitude. One of the most unexpected moments was when Sheryl and Dave, the race directors, announced the winners of the three awards that reinforce the main principles of the Hawaiian culture and the spirit of the Ultraman: Aloha — love, Kokua — help, and Ohana — family.

Team Luz crossing the finish line in the Ultraman World Championship – Hawaii
— Photo by Matthew D'Avella

Sheryl started by saying "We have seen this group grow over the years, especially the kids …" She got my attention, as it really took us a couple of years to cross the Ultraman finish line. Sheryl then continued, "And this group has experienced both sides. Their athlete sometimes was successful, other times he was not." Oh yes, the story started to sound familiar. She then concluded, "… But independent of the result or of the difficulties they faced in the race, they aways showed up with a big smile, and they were certainly having a lot of fun. That's the spirit of the Ultraman. The Ohana Award goes to the Da Luz Family!"

Jai, Tata, and the kids were surprised by the announcement, while the crowd erupted into cheers. Justice was done, and they got the award and a plate much bigger than my finisher medal. They earned it!

To finish, every athlete gets the stage for a three-minute speech. Some will tell their own journey, what led them to the Big Island; others will share details of the race. I used the time just to thank the people who had been an inspiration and support for me along the way. Of course, three minutes were not enough, and a speech at the remote Kona Old Airport venue may be forgotten, but maybe I could find a different way to recognize these exceptional people.

Team Luz with the Ohana Award

*Ultraman World
Championship medal*

CHAPTER 18

IT IS NOT ABOUT
WHAT YOU SAY

"The world is changed by examples, not by opinions."
—*Paulo Coelho, Brazilian author*

2023 TO 24

With my result at the Ultraman, I also qualified for the US Nationals, the second opportunity I had to race at a Nationals championship. The first one, when I was part of the Stanford triathlon team, I decided to pass because I didn't want to be away from Jai and the kids for the race. Eight years later, things had changed, and I was not the only one to qualify for the competitive Nationals this time.

With all the races and training to get ready for the Ultraman, triathlon became a recurrent topic in the family dinners, and eventually Jai and Sophia decided to also venture into the chilly waters of Santa Cruz, California. They bravely swam among the seals, sea lions, and sea otters over the kelp forests of Monterey Bay, rode under a lot of heat, and ran the rolling hills of the rugged California coast to complete their first triathlon. They were bold!

We switched places, and I was the one cheering them on, following them around the course and trying to capture the best moments of their experience. Both did great, and Sophia, who was sixteen and nervous before the race, many times yelling at me for having suggested a "nonsense race," ended up in third place and qualified for US Nationals, right on her first triathlon! It took me ten years to qualify for one, and I was glad it happened the same year that it did for Sophia.

As we trained for the Nationals together, Gabe decided to join us on a prep race. His nervousness leading up to the race was evident. Although I never pushed anyone to race, I was the one to blame for the "unnecessary big challenge" ahead, and my "ideas" had gotten him in trouble, but after swimming the calm waters of the Russian River, riding through the beautiful landscape of the Sonoma Wine Country, and flying on the run course (it was hard to keep up with him), Gabe completed his first triathlon at the age of twelve and was the personification of happiness and exhaustion in the end.

Triathlon not only played a major role in my personal growth and transformation, it also became a strong part of the story that got me accepted into Stanford. Sophia built her own triathlon stories and reflected on her experiences and learnings in the college application process. Along with strong schoolwork and extracurricular activities, triathlon helped her get into many top colleges. She chose UC Berkeley, which, by twist of fate, is Stanford's biggest rival in sports. But we have no rivalry at home; Jai and I are incredibly proud of her and will always be her biggest fans.

Whether they continue to do triathlons or not is up to them. Maybe they will find something else more interesting. Gabe loves soccer and continue to progress well there. In three years, he moved from the fourth team of the soccer club of our town to the first team, and this year he was also selected to join the school soccer team. We are also very proud of him and will always be his biggest fans.

It was never about triathlons. It was about learning the importance of keeping an active life and that, with the right preparation, they can take on any big challenge.

*Gabe and Sophia after their triathlon
in Sonoma, CA, 2024*

*Exhausted but happy kids,
Sonoma, CA, 2024*

*Gabe riding his bike during the race,
Sonoma, CA, 2024*

*Sophia on the podium in
her first triathlon,
Santa Cruz, CA, 2023*

Jai and Sophia on their first triathlon in Santa Cruz, CA, 2023

6k run with the kids, Tata, and Andre (running his first half marathon), Nova Friburgo, Brazil, 2018

Kids' Run at California International Marathon, Sacramento, CA, 2018

IronKids in Santa Rosa, CA, 2017

Ironman 70.3 Santa Cruz, CA, 2016

Ironkids in Syracuse, NY, 2015

Sophia placed 2nd and Gabe 3rd in the Wildflower sprint triathlon, California, 2025

Celebrating a summer tournament win,
Belmont, CA, 2023

10k Run in San Francisco, CA, 2022

Go Stanford! Go Bears!
Belmont, CA, 2025

At the US Nationals, 2023

CHAPTER 19

WRITING TO MYSELF

"It always seems impossible until it is done."
—*Nelson Mandela, South African anti-apartheid revolutionary*

2024

The journey from a sedentary life to the lava fields of Hawaii has been beyond belief, however, for me, the main achievement in this entire process was not completing my first marathon, Ironman, or the Ultraman World Championship. It was not losing and keeping off over eighty pounds, entering one of the most prestigious universities in the world, or giving my family rich experiences of character, willpower, and resilience. Overcoming childhood challenges and limitations to produce this book is at the top of the list.

At four years old, I skipped a school year. At six years old, I moved to a large school where each class had more than forty students, all older than me. A dyslexic kid learns better in small classes and is normally a late bloomer. If anything, it is probably better to be a year behind the other kids, not ahead. Early school years were hard socially. On the academic front, reading and writing were the Ultraman of my early years. Those are typical challenges for any dyslexic kid; imagine being in a giant classroom having to catch up with older kids. But in the midst of this sink-or-swim scenario, I had a lifeline.

Right before moving schools, my kindergarten teacher, Miss Daisy (Tia Margarida), approached my mom and let her know that her son needed help. I was not able to learn the difference between some letters, such as P and B, or F and V; I would also mirror some letters and could not pronounce some phonemes, especially the ones with R. I was lucky to have a teacher not only with the best possible name for a kindergarten teacher but one who deeply cared about her little students. More than forty years ago, it would have been easy to just label me "slow" or "dumb" and move on. Nowadays, those labels are not socially accepted; they have been replaced by others that come accompanied by doctors' prescriptions. Miss Daisy understood what I needed at that time, went above and beyond to give me individualized support, and recommended to my mom that I start speech therapy right away.

My earliest childhood memories are of annoying my sister, Tata, to get her attention (something I think I still do today), fishing with my dad, who would sleep for most of the time (something he still does today), and going to speech therapy with my mom, who deeply cared about me. Things don't seem to change much over time. Battling financial challenges and the disbelief of my dad, my mom would take me to speech therapy sessions two to three times a week, and it helped me tremendously. I was able to keep up with schoolwork, and I believe the speech issues were fixed before they were noticed; at least I don't remember being bullied for it, which is a good sign. My mom says that swimming helped a lot back then; the way she describes it is that it would help calm me and get things more organized. It still does today. I was lucky to have had Miss Daisy and a caring mom to help me through the early years, but not everyone has similar circumstances. I think things are even worse nowadays because the new normal is just to legally drug the kids who are different, so they can fit into the standards of academic life. The irony is that in professional life, things take a turn. Employers often ask, "I have all these resumes that look the same. What differentiates you?"

Last year, I was talking with a friend who has a child with dyslexia and is on various medications. We talked for a while, and she then said, "I need to give him the medicine; any day that I forget, the teacher sends a message complaining." The medicine works on the kids' reward system, artificially releasing dopamine so the kid can concentrate on tasks that are harder and need more attention. Do you know what is a great natural source for dopamine? Exercise, with the extra benefit of also loading the brain with endorphins, serotonin, adrenaline, and many other import- ant hormones that help the person be happier, smarter, stronger, and more motivated to do things. Why not just let a kid be who he was born to be and use sports to develop the social skills needed to integrate into society? Having lived through this experience myself, I believe it will work for almost everyone.

Despite all the effort from my mom and from Marly, my speech therapist, reading continued to be a huge challenge for me as a kid. From K–12, I never read a book outside of school, and even for schoolwork, the reading was minimal. I'd read just a summary of the book, the first and last pages, or just talk to someone to learn what the book's story was, and like that, I'd survive the exams along the way. Consequently, writing was bad too. I was always in the remedial classes, and I grew up convinced that reading and writing were not for me. One of the reasons I chose engineering as a career was that there was nearly no reading and absolutely no writing.

Things started to change when I entered the job market. Emails, memos, faxes, and letters were my business cards, and I didn't think it would be smart to send something badly written. Sometimes it would take me hours to get the text right, but I would not compromise; that was my career. To my surprise, on my first internship at a Brazilian oil company, I was put in charge of writing marketing promotion announcements to the sales teams. They were business documents, and for me, it was a matter of organizing information so it could be consumed easily. They are direct, simple to understand, but cold. When applying to Stanford many years later, I knew things needed to be different; it was not about the information in the essay but about the emotions. How to spark emotions in the reader that would make him or her remember my story, knowing that they would not remember any of the details of it. It took me almost a year to get there, but I didn't give up. I knew I had hit the mark when my wife's feedback after reading yet another draft was, "I'm in tears."

At Stanford, I started to like writing a bit, and for the first time in my life, I had a writing class that I enjoyed. I was always looking forward to attending "Winning Writing" with Professor Glenn Kramon. Being a school alum himself, Glenn always started the classes with old pictures and tales of the farm, then moved to pragmatic writing lessons, often hard, but fun. It was the first time I wrote about my experience with cycling. I didn't like what I wrote, but Glenn did. He encouraged me to continue writing, even used the word "fascinating" in his feedback, but I didn't do that, not at that time.

The leap from a two-page essay or writing exercise to a two-hundred-page book was not an easy one, but if it were easy, it would not be interesting. It took me five years to complete the Ultraman World Championship. The book took longer than that, but the process was fantastic. I got to relive life-changing experiences, reconnect with people who have been important to me, and once again, I believe I was lucky to share the journey with extraordinary individuals who were willing to dedicate precious time from their lives to read early rough drafts and provide feedback along the way.

I started writing about the races to myself, almost like a race report, and it was interesting. To write, I had to revisit the race, what happened during the race, and what happened before the race. It made it easier for me to connect many dots on why things were unfolding the way they did. I found writing to be a powerful healing process.

The early messy drafts got better, and I started sharing with some people who were close to me. They liked the content, but there were opportunities to improve the writing style. *Could I make it more interesting for the reader?* After a long ride, I decided to write about day two of Ultraman Canada. It was a turning point; people felt engaged, and they "pedaled with me" in Canada. *Could I then turn those stories into chapters and the chapters into a book?* As it always is in life, after a milestone, there is always another one, and hopefully, there will be a lot of learning in between them. I had to learn a lot before I could produce something that could be interesting for people to read, like many books were for me on my own journey.

In an earlier chapter, I talked about how *Finding Ultra*, a memoir from Stanford alum Rich Roll, helped me in my own personal journey. There were many other similar memoirs that helped me along the way, including *Eat and Run*, *North*, *Born to Run*, *Ultramarathon Man*, *Can't Hurt Me*, and *Open*, to mention a few. I learned a lot from each book and became inspired by their unique stories. I'm thankful for the fact that these people took the risk to become authors and shared their experiences with the world. I believe that the best way to give back to this community was to take the same risk and hope to return the favor by letting the stories in this book inspire others.

CHAPTER 20

A HOST OF ANGELS

"The two most important days in your life are the day you are born and the day you find out why."

—*Mark Twain, American author*

ALWAYS

I t doesn't matter what dream you have—a crazy race, a prestigious school, a challenging career, an adventurous trip, a big recital, or just transforming yourself—there are two things I hope for you. First, that your dream is big enough to scare you, to make you wake up many days questioning if it is really possible, to make you occasionally regret having dreamed that big, because those are the dreams that push us forward. They force us to learn and create different things; they keep us living, not just surviving, in this world. Second, I hope you surround yourself with great people who will help you get there. It makes all the difference in the world, and I can attest to that.

It would not have been possible to do what I did without the strong support from the people close to me. The amazing partnership with Jai, who supported me, joined the races, and kept our home and family united and functioning well. The great support from Sophia and Gabe, who trained a lot with me and would always cheer at the races, not to mention their great contribution in reading, laughing, and criticizing this book along the way. I'm not a native English speaker; they are. Tata, who would cross half of the planet just to be with the kids for a few days and to race with me. She did it for the first half marathon in Philly, back in 2013, all the way to the Ultraman Hawaii in 2023. There were many other angels along the way.

Dani, of course, the crazy one who took up the challenge to start running in the winter and was faster than me, pushing me to the limits in the races. No, I haven't beat him—yet. Yon was not only a crewmember for my first two Ultraman races but started running with me and one day asked me to teach him how to swim. At that moment, I realized that I had great swimming skills but little knowledge. The only thing I could say to him in the pool was, "Do you see the border on the other side? Get there. And don't drown, please." He hired a swimming coach after that. Dario and Fabio, friends from Brazil, were following my training and races from a distance, asking tons of questions, and making suggestions. They both started running marathons and kept an active life after that.

I also really enjoyed sharing with others what I had learned. Sandro, who when we first met told me that he had given up on running, as every time he tried, a major injury would come up. After running together a few times, he got the technique right and has run many races injury free since then, including the 70.3 Ironman in Hawaii. Gonzalo, a friend who battled some health issues and believed he could not ride up a mountain, but bravely teamed up with David and Fabien and made up to the top of Old La Honda, a classic climb near the Stanford campus. His happiness that day was contagious, and he started mountain biking after that. Like them, there have been countless first-time runners, cyclists, and triathletes that I have helped get started in the sport, overcome challenges, or simply showed them some beautiful places or routes to train. Helping them helped me continue to be motivated and engaged.

Some angels appeared at special moments, like the Healer when I thought the IT band syndrome was incurable; Dr. Jesus, who helped build my confidence before Ironman Cozumel; Slava, shaking up my crew at Ultraman Florida; and Suzy and Doug at Ultraman Hawaii. Steve King, the voice of Ultraman, was always there, appearing like an angel in the most remote places, with his mic and unbelievable knowledge about every athlete and crew, giving us a much-needed boost to keep going. Sheryl, David, and Jane, the race directors for Ultraman Hawaii, who keep the spirit of the race alive, supporting all athletes and crew members every step of the way. They were all exceptional. Aloha. Ohana. Kokua.

Of course, there is Rob, who I learn more from during a lunch hour than in years of training and races. As I mentioned Rob in the book a couple of times, I sent him an early draft so he could review it. He said that he had a lot of fun reading it, but had some feedback for me, not on the book, but on the training:

"In the book you used the word 'sprinting' down the hill, which I'm hoping might just be an expression, because you should never be sprinting, just running a quick pace. If you really did sprint, for sure the recovery would be even longer." Oh yes, I was sprinting, and this may explain a thing or two. Thankfully, learning is never over in life.

There were also many angels to help me author the book. Glenn sparked the idea back at the Stanford writing class, encouraging me to go deeper. My mom, Celia, and my mother-in-law, Angela, read every piece that I wrote and loved it, but they were biased. My Stanford friend Ali, a best-selling author, was way more critical. She didn't want to see any of the drafts; instead, she asked for the chapter plan. Of course, I didn't have one. I developed one, and she told me, in her polite Welsh way, that it was all wrong because I was trying to fit a couple of books into one. Eventually, I got that straightened up. Dalton, one of the smartest people I have met, helped a lot. After reading an early draft, he called me and said, "Hey, man, there is an interesting story there, but as we know each other, I'm going to focus what needs to get better," and there were a lot of things. His main feedback was on how each chapter was organized. They didn't have a specific focus. I reorganized them, included the quotes to help guide the readers, and the book became easier to follow. He also helped with some of the book's transitions, language, and more.

Dario, the only nonfamily member who read everything I had written, made me scratch nearly one hundred pages before sharing with other people because he didn't feel the same empathy for those pages as he did for the first part of the book. He was right and saved a lot of other friends from reading something that was not interesting. Sergio, an elementary school friend and Ironman, immediately related the draft of the first chapter to the movie *Cool Runnings*, which helped include some comedic twists in the book, keeping it light. Fernanda, another elementary school friend and author, was caught by the family relationships in the drafts and helped me include more emotion in the book, making it more meaningful. She also didn't hold back. I still remember her feedback on the initial drafts. "You write very well, there are a lot of good things in the stories"—certainly a preface to strong feedback—"but there are too many details. It reads more like a diary. You will need to rewrite everything." I knew she was right, and I did rewrite it, after all. They all helped me significantly dial back the level of detail in the book and make it more interesting.

Michael, who helped thousands of people believe in their future by teaching them how to code, also helped me believe in my book by engaging since its early drafts. Antonio, who has also impacted thousands of lives with his ventures and social impact documentary film, helped me craft the way I would tell the different stories and recommended a great book, *Story* by Robert McKee, where I learned that a "scene [or story, in this case] is never about what the scene is about." Chapter 1 is not about a hard race day, but resilience; chapter 2 is not about a promotion, but family, and so on. This chapter is not about angels, but gratitude. This book is not about triathlon, but personal growth and transformation that I hope can help others in their own journeys.

One day, on a long ride, I ran into some delays while trying to help my wife block all her credit cards because she had lost her wallet. I was at the shore, over two hours riding from home, and I miscalculated the time needed to bike back. Night fell, and I ended up stranded on the west side of the Santa Cruz Mountains without any light. It was too dark to ride, so I stopped on the shoulder and started to check my dying phone, hoping for a signal, but no luck—I was in the middle of nowhere. Suddenly, a minivan showed up. I was not in the mood for a creepy ride, but when they opened the window, there was a young couple with three talkative kids inside; the oldest was probably five, and they were all curious about me. The Stanford triathlon cycling kit probably gave them the comfort level to offer me a ride. I took it. We were about an hour's drive from home, with plenty of time to talk. And they wanted to talk. The dad asked me, "So, my wife and I were having a discussion, and some outside perspective could help, especially coming from someone who has gone through Stanford."

Oh my God, what did I get myself into?

He then continued, "I'm not going to say who is in which camp so we don't influence you, but one of us thinks that our older daughter should skip the last year of preschool and go straight to kindergarten. The other one of us doesn't agree with that. We have this unique opportunity, as one of her grandfathers is the director of a prestigious private school." The topic could not be closer to my heart.

I replied, "Your daughter has seven years of childhood, from five to twelve. Are you sure you want to steal nearly 15 percent of that? She will be forced to mature a year earlier, choose a profession a year earlier, start working a year earlier, and date a year earlier. Are you sure this is a clever idea?" Silence took over the car; not even the talkative kids were talking. I then continued, "I have experienced it myself; I skipped a year, and to this day, I'm sure parents have the best intentions when they do that, but it is hard to believe that shortening a kid's childhood can help him or her."

The couple looked at each other, and the dad replied, "We had never thought of it that way, but you know what? It makes sense!" I never asked who was in each camp. It didn't matter; I was happy I could help a kid have a normal childhood. The ride was supposed to be to the point where I could get a signal and call an Uber or my wife, but they insisted on taking me home, an additional hour for them. It's hard to know who was more of an angel to whom that night.

I believe that the best way to attract awesome angels into your life is to be a good angel yourself. What goes around comes around, and my hope is that the stories in this book inspire you not only to find great angels for your life but also to become an angel for many others.

When things were not going well at work, at home, or with myself, it was hard to have big dreams or to think of helping others. The day-to-day stress would consume me, until that fall of 2013, when I decided to go for a run. I haven't stopped since then. If you are unsure of what to do or how to start, go for a run. And never stop running!

*With Doug before the UMWC award
ceremony, Kona, HI, 2023*

*With Suzy right after the completion
of UMWC, Kona, HI, 2023*

One of the many calls with Rob, 2023

*With Steve King at the completion
of Ultraman Florida,
Clermont, FL, 2020*

With Antonio, David, and Fabien on West Old La Honda, Woodside, 2017

With Dario, catching up in Rio de Janeiro, 2024

Dani recovering from a marathon while I was leaving for Ironman Cozumel, Chadds Ford, PA, 2014

Running a marathon in Delaware with Yon, 2016

At the top of Old La Honda with Gonzalo, Fabien, and David, Woodside, CA, 2017

With Sandro, his wife Michelle, and Sophia at Ironman 70.3, Santa Cruz, CA, 2023

Enjoying Rio with Dalton and our families, 2023

Walking the Stanford Dish with Michael, 2017

Rio de Janeiro Marathon with Fabio, 2014

Riding the Portola Loop with Glenn and other Stanford students, Woodside, CA, 2017

*With Serginho. Pictures taken
40 years apart*

*With Fernanda and friends
from K-12 school:
Roberta, Carlos, Marcelo, Tatiana,
Eduardo, and Walter after our 30-year
high school graduation party,
Rio de Janeiro, 2023*

*Catching up with Rodrigo after
reading Joel Fiel's book,
The Triathlete's Training Bible*

*With Jane, also known as "Ultra Mama,"
at the 2023 awards ceremony
in Kona, HI*

Team Luz with Sheryl and David at the 2023 awards ceremony
in Kona, HI

IM Santa Rosa Celebration with amazing support crew and a lot
of future champs! Shirley, Gabriel, Jai, Sophia, Stella, Bia, Yon,
Marcel, Fernando, Alan, Abhnay, Tiessa, and Jonas! Santa Rosa, CA